Mahmoud Darwish

Dalya Cohen-Mor

Mahmoud Darwish

Palestine's Poet and the Other as the Beloved

Dalya Cohen-Mor
Potomac, MD, USA

ISBN 978-3-030-24161-2   ISBN 978-3-030-24162-9   (eBook)
https://doi.org/10.1007/978-3-030-24162-9

© The Editor(s) (if applicable) and The Author(s), under exclusive licence to Springer
Nature Switzerland AG 2019
This work is subject to copyright. All rights are solely and exclusively licensed by the
Publisher, whether the whole or part of the material is concerned, specifically the rights
of translation, reprinting, reuse of illustrations; recitation, broadcasting, reproduction
on microfilms or in any other physical way, and transmission or information storage and
retrieval, electronic adaptation, computer software, or by similar or dissimilar methodology
now known or hereafter developed.
The use of general descriptive names, registered names, trademarks, service marks, etc. in this
publication does not imply, even in the absence of a specific statement, that such names are
exempt from the relevant protective laws and regulations and therefore free for general use.
The publisher, the authors and the editors are safe to assume that the advice and
information in this book are believed to be true and accurate at the date of publication.
Neither the publisher nor the authors or the editors give a warranty, expressed or implied,
with respect to the material contained herein or for any errors or omissions that may have
been made. The publisher remains neutral with regard to jurisdictional claims in published
maps and institutional affiliations.

Cover credit: © Harvey Loake

This Palgrave Pivot imprint is published by the registered company Springer Nature
Switzerland AG
The registered company address is: Gewerbestrasse 11, 6330 Cham, Switzerland

PREFACE

This study focuses on the Palestinian national poet Mahmoud Darwish (1941–2008), whose poetry has helped to shape Palestinian identity and foster Palestinian culture through many decades of the Israeli–Palestinian conflict. The study explores the poet's romantic relationship with "Rita," an Israeli-Jewish woman whom he had met in Haifa in his early twenties and to whom he had dedicated a series of love poems and prose passages, among them the iconic poem "Rita and the Gun." These love poems and prose passages open a window into an intimate chapter in Darwish's life that left a lasting mark on his creative work. Interwoven with biographical details and diverse documentary materials, this exploration reveals a fascinating facet in the poet's personality, his self-definition, and his attitude toward the Israeli other. Comprising a close reading of Darwish's love poems, coupled with many examples of novels and short stories from both Arabic and Hebrew fiction that deal with Arab-Jewish love stories, this study delves into the complexity of Arab-Jewish relations and shows how romance can blossom across ethno-religious lines and how politics all too often destroys it.

Chapter 1 *The Poet's Public Persona: A Lover from Palestine* introduces Mahmoud Darwish to the reader, presenting the major events of his life and the main stages in his poetic career. I discuss the characteristic features of Darwish's political poetry, focusing on his use of the beloved as a metaphor for Palestine or the land, for which he became known as "a lover from Palestine." This public image led to a tendency among Arab readers and critics alike to construe every love poem that he wrote

v

vi PREFACE

as a poem for the homeland. Given this tendency, as well as the ongoing Palestinian struggle for liberation from Israeli occupation, the Rita poems, dedicated to an Israeli-Jewish woman with whom Darwish had a passionate love affair, were largely shrouded in silence and mystery or else interpreted metaphorically.

Chapter 2 *Dangerous Liaisons: Arab-Jewish Romantic Relationships* provides background information on interfaith dating and marriage in Israel to contextualize the complications surrounding Darwish's love affair with Rita. I look at the prevailing social attitudes toward this issue, the existing laws, and the statistics on both sides of the ethno-religious divide. Regarded as an act of treason by members of both Arab and Jewish societies, interfaith romance and marriage are discouraged and incur great hardships for couples who violate this taboo. The situation on the ground is mirrored in works of fiction by both Arab and Jewish authors in Israel, and I present many examples of novels and short stories that depict such relationships, almost all of which end in heartache, breakup, or death.

Chapter 3 *Self-Defining Memories: When Mahmoud Met "Rita"* describes the forbidden love between Darwish and Rita. Drawing on multiple sources, including the recent documentary film *Write Down, I Am an Arab* (*Sajjil ana 'Arabi*), newspaper articles, and published interviews, I provide an account of Rita's identity, background, and career, how she and Darwish met, what brought them together, and what drove them apart. I offer an explanation as to why, following their breakup, Rita became a leitmotif in Darwish's poetry. I highlight the power of first love as the main motive for this leitmotif, and also draw on the theory of "self-defining memories" in psychology to elucidate its function. This theory is particularly pertinent here, given that Darwish's love for Rita was unrequited and ended in heartache.

Chapter 4 *The Rita Love Poems and Prose Passages* offers a close reading of the love poems and prose passages that Darwish dedicated to Rita over a period of twenty-five years, from 1967 to 1992. I discuss dominant themes, images, and messages. I draw a comparison between the impossible love of Darwish and Rita and that of other famous lovers in literature, the Arab Qais and Layla and the European Romeo and Juliet, all of whom belonged to hostile/warring groups. Finally, I offer an explanation as to why Rita ceased to appear in Darwish's poetry from the end of 1992 until his death in 2008.

Chapter 5 *Unbeliever in the Impossible* examines the implications of the most celebrated love story between a Palestinian man and an Israeli-Jewish woman in recent history. What does it reveal about Darwish's self-definition and his attitude toward the Israeli other? I argue that although Darwish came to be known as a poet of resistance, he had always advocated dialogue with Israelis and embraced the Israeli component in his Palestinian identity, as evidenced by the facts that he spoke Hebrew fluently and read and appreciated the poetry of Israel's national poet Hayim Nahman Bialik and Israel's greatest modern poet Yehuda Amichai. The personal story of these star-crossed lovers is ultimately a metaphor for Arab-Jewish relations. It illustrates the tragedy of two neighboring communities that have the potential to develop close and enriching ties but are instead embroiled in a century-long conflict. Darwish's resonant words, "We are both unbelievers in the impossible," which he wrote in one of his love poems, offer a message of hope that this seemingly unresolvable conflict will someday come to an end.

Potomac, MD, USA   Dalya Cohen-Mor

RITA AND THE GUN

Between Rita and my eyes is a gun
and whoever knows Rita kneels
and prays
to some divinity in those hazel eyes.

And I kissed Rita
when she was young
and I remember how she clung to me
and how my arm was covered by the loveliest of braids
and I remember Rita
as a sparrow remembers its stream.
Ah, Rita
between us are a million sparrows and pictures
and countless trysts
fired on ... by a gun.

Rita's name was a feast in my mouth
Rita's body was a wedding in my blood
and I was lost in Rita for two years
and for two years she slept on my arm
and we made pledges over the most beautiful of cups
and we burned in the wine of our lips
and we were born again.

Ah, Rita
what made my eyes turn from yours
but a couple of brief naps

and hazel clouds
in a time before this gun.

Once upon a time ...
O silence of the evening
my moon migrated far in the morning
in the hazel eyes
and the city
swept away all the singers and Rita.
Between Rita and my eyes is a gun.

From *Selected Poems: Mahmoud Darwish*. Introduced and translated by Ian Wedde and Fawwaz Tuqan. Cheadle Hulme, UK: Carcanet Press, 1973. Copyright © 1973 by Ian Wedde. Revised by Ian Wedde. Reprinted by permission of Ian Wedde.

CONTENTS

1 The Poet's Public Persona: A Lover from Palestine   1

2 Dangerous Liaisons: Arab-Jewish Romantic Relationships   13

3 Self-Defining Memories: When Mahmoud Met "Rita"   45

4 The Rita Love Poems and Prose Passages   65

5 Unbeliever in the Impossible   83

Bibliography   95

Index   101

CHAPTER 1

The Poet's Public Persona: A Lover from Palestine

Abstract This chapter introduces Mahmoud Darwish to the reader, presenting the major stages in his life and poetic career. I discuss the characteristics of Darwish's political poetry, focusing on his use of the beloved as a metaphor for Palestine, for which he became known as "a lover from Palestine." This public image led to a tendency among Arab readers and critics alike to construe every love poem that he wrote as a poem for the homeland. Given this tendency, and the ongoing Palestinian struggle for liberation from Israeli occupation, the Rita poems, dedicated to an Israeli-Jewish woman with whom Darwish had a passionate love affair, were largely shrouded in silence and mystery or else interpreted metaphorically.

Keywords Palestine—national poet—Mahmoud Darwish · Mahmoud Darwish—public persona · Mahmoud Darwish—political poetry · Mahmoud Darwish—love poems

"We are captives of what we love, what we desire, and what we are" writes Mahmoud Darwish in his poem "The Hoopoe."[1] This memorable line offers a fascinating insight into his life and work as Palestine's national poet. Formed by the experience of occupation, imprisonment, and exile, Darwish strove in his poems to shape and foster Palestinian identity and culture. His love for his lost homeland and the desire to preserve its memory in the

© The Author(s) 2019
D. Cohen-Mor, *Mahmoud Darwish,*
https://doi.org/10.1007/978-3-030-24162-9_1

1

consciousness of his people motivated much of his writing and yielded a remarkable output of lyrical poetry. In poem after poem, Darwish spoke of his deep attachment to Palestine, its towns, its landscape, its flora and fauna. The pinnacle of his emotional connection to the land found its expression in the poem "Diary of Palestinian Wound," in which he said: "Ah my intractable wound! / My country is not a suitcase / I am not a traveler / I am the lover and the land is the beloved."[2] Blending nationalist verse with love poetry, he created a new kind of patriotic poem in Arabic, or a new kind of love poem, in which Palestine is fused with the figure of the beloved and is the object of erotic attention.[3]

Erotic love as a metaphor for attachment to the homeland is vividly depicted in "A Lover from Palestine," the title poem of Darwish's third collection (published in 1966), in which the poet-speaker says to his beloved: "Your eyes are a thorn in the heart / It pains me, yet I adore it."[4] In this poem, Palestine is depicted as the idealized beloved with "Palestinian eyes," "a Palestinian name," "Palestinian dreams and sorrows," "Palestinian veil, feet, and body," "Palestinian words and silence," "a Palestinian birth and death."[5] Sensual and evocative, the poem expresses the poet's longing to be united with his homeland in intimate, almost mystical terms. "Take me wherever you are," he pleads with his beloved. "Restore to me the color of face / And the warmth of body, / The light of heart and eye, / The salt of bread and rhythm, / The taste of earth … the Motherland."[6]

"The eroticization of the land provides a metaphor for belonging that approximates the intimacy, passion, and emotional turmoil of romantic relationships," notes the literary scholar Khaled Mattawa.[7] Many of Darwish's patriotic poems speak of unrequited love and a painful separation from his beloved. At times the land is portrayed as a mysterious, idolized female, visible but inaccessible to her tormented lover. At other times it is depicted as a seductive woman who captivates the poet with her charms but bestows her favors on others: "Your lips are honey, and your hands / glasses of wine / for others."[8] Despite the beloved's lack of attention, the poet remains loyal and devoted to her, stating unequivocally: "I will love your nectar / even though it is poured into the glasses of others."[9] In the long run, however, having been banished from his beloved and unable to communicate with her, the denied lover becomes dispirited. Acknowledging his bad luck, he says: "I am the unlucky lover / One narcissus is for me and another against me."[10] Although Darwish's poetry has evolved over the years and transcended the limits of patriotic and resistance poems, the role of "a lover from Palestine" ("'Ashiq min Filastin") became his public persona, to the extent that even a personal poem such as "To My Mother," which expresses his nostalgia for his mother's bread and coffee, was interpreted as a poem for the motherland.[11] Set to music by the Lebanese musician Marcel Khalife, it continues to be sung by thousands of Palestinians as a national hymn for their homeland.

Mahmoud Darwish was born on 13 March 1941 into a lower middle-class Muslim family in the village of al-Birwa, east of Acre, in northern Palestine. His family fled to Lebanon during the 1948 Arab-Israeli war, and by the time they returned to their village, about a year later, it had been razed and a kibbutz had been built on its site. Because the family was absent in 1949, when the first census was taken in Israel, and thus not counted in it, they were considered "infiltrators" or illegal residents when they returned, which meant that they could not obtain an ID and could be deported if discovered. They lived in the village of Deir al-Assad (6 mi east of al-Birwa), hiding their presence from the authorities for three years, until they received the necessary papers. In 1963 they moved to the village of al-Jadida, a few miles west of their native village of al-Birwa.[12]

The displacement, exile, and loss of their property and means of livelihood came as a great blow to the Darwish family, which experienced a profound economic and psychological crisis. The Palestinian scholar Muna Abu Eid notes that Darwish, who was a seven-year-old boy when his family fled to Lebanon, discovered at that time the meaning of "homeland" (*watan*), a concept that later became pivotal in his life and poetry. As she elaborates: "Return became his daily bread: the return to the place, the return to time, the return from the temporary to the permanent, the return from the present to both the past and the future, the return from the unusual to the natural, the return from tin boxes to a house of stone. Thus, Palestine became the opposite of everything else, and became a lost paradise."[13] Darwish depicts the trauma of his family's flight to Lebanon and their return from there in the poems "The Eternity of Cactus" and "To My End and to Its End," both of which appear in his collection *Why Did You Leave the Horse Alone?*, which is regarded as his autobiographical volume.[14]

As a young boy, Darwish showed interest in painting, music, and poetry. It has been suggested that he became a poet rather than a painter because his family lacked the financial means to buy him the supplies needed for drawing and painting. The father, a farmer who became a quarry worker, had difficulties providing for his family. Mahmoud was the second of his eight children, five boys and three girls. There was no tradition of writing

4 D. COHEN-MOR

poems in Darwish's family, although his older brother Ahmad, and his grandfather, who was a dominant figure in his childhood, encouraged him to write.

After completing elementary school in Deir al-Assad, Darwish attended the Arab high school in Kafr Yasif (1956–1960), then a center of Arab national and political activity and a stronghold of the Israeli Communist Party. In addition to his studies in Arabic, he was also taught the Hebrew language, Hebrew literature, and the Bible. Darwish acknowledged the influence of these subjects on his development as a poet. He was exposed not only to works of poetry and prose in Hebrew but also to works of world literature translated into Hebrew. "I am grateful," he said, "to Hebrew that opened for me a window into foreign literatures."[15] Alongside the inspiration he drew from both classical and modern Arabic poetry, he read and appreciated the poems of Israel's national poet Hayim Nahman Bialik (1873–1934) and Israel's greatest modern poet Yehuda Amichai (1924–2000).

Darwish did not pursue higher education after graduating from high school; instead, he spent two years in Acre, where he worked at an Arabic printing press. In 1962 he moved to Haifa and started working for the Israeli Communist Party's Arabic newspapers, *al-Jadid* and *al-Ittihad*, where he published his poems. Like many Palestinian intellectuals at the time, he joined the party not for ideological reasons but because it was the only political framework that gave legitimacy to the expression of Palestinian national sentiments. There he met the Palestinian leaders of the party, the author Emile Habibi (1922–1996), Emile Touma (1919–1985), and Tawfiq Toubi (1922–2011), all of whom had a great influence on his development as a poet and as an intellectual.

Darwish spent ten productive years in Haifa during which he honed his poetic and journalistic skills. Along with the poet Samih al-Qasim (1939–2014), he lived in the house of Emile Touma, who was one of the editors of *al-Ittihad*. In Haifa he belonged to a group of Arab and Jewish poets who, under the sponsorship of the Israeli Communist Party, met together to read poetry and discuss peaceful coexistence. Although during those years he also experienced imprisonment and house arrest, it was, by his own account, one of the happiest periods of his life: it helped him shape his national consciousness, define his cultural identity, and establish himself as a poet and a journalist.[16] It was during this time, too, that he met and fell in love with Tamar Ben-Ami, alias Rita.

1 THE POET'S PUBLIC PERSONA: A LOVER FROM PALESTINE   5

In the decade between 1960 and 1970, the first stage of his poetic career, Darwish published eight volumes of poetry, gaining the reputation of a poet of resistance and the voice of the Palestinian people. The most famous poem of this period is "Identity Card" ("Bitaqat huwiyya"), published in his first volume *Olive Leaves* in 1964. It is a monologue delivered by a stone quarrier who confronts an Israeli official. Composed of five stanzas, each of which begins with the words "Write down / I am an Arab," the poem tells of the quarrier's hard life and family history, ending with a warning directed at the Israeli official: "Beware, beware of my hunger / and of my anger."[17] The poem achieved enormous popularity for its spirit of defiance and for its assertion of Arab identity in the face of a hostile authority. Critics have wondered why Darwish wrote "I am an Arab" and not "I am a Palestinian." However, prior to the 1967 Arab-Israeli war Palestinians living in Israel did not define themselves as Palestinians but as Arabs.[18] Critics have also wondered what language the quarrier is speaking, assuming that it must be Arabic since he defines himself as an Arab. But in his book *Memory for Forgetfulness* (published in 1986), Darwish discusses the origins of this poem and claims that the refrain "Write down, I am an Arab" was a phrase in Hebrew that he once said to an Israeli official in order to provoke him.[19] Choosing to articulate these words in Hebrew reflects Darwish's sensitivity to the nuanced relationship between language and power.[20] The refrain "Write down / I am an Arab" (sajjil ana 'arabi) was fifty years later adopted as the title of an award-winning documentary film about Mahmoud Darwish by Ibtisam Mara'ana-Menuhin.

Despite the poem's continued popularity throughout the years—it is still recited in public and widely applauded by Arab audiences—Darwish was not fond of it, perhaps because of its straightforward statements and declamatory tone. In an interview he said, "I can't stand this poem, 'Identity Card.' I tried to remove it from my collected works but it has become so deeply rooted in the hearts of readers that I couldn't oppose it and therefore I gave in."[21] This dilemma demonstrates the complicated position of the poet who is made into a spokesman for his people and must decide how to navigate his relationship with his public. Darwish faced this dilemma throughout his poetic career.

As noted earlier, the characteristic feature of Darwish's poems at this first stage is the "eroticization of the land," that is, the fusion of the homeland with the beloved: "It is her streams, springs, and mountains that are the objects of the poet's love, and he lends them human attributes" says the literary critic Robyn Creswell.[22] In "The Most Beautiful Love," for example, the beloved is an allegorical figure for Palestine, to whom the poet professes his love: "I love you as travelers in a desert love an oasis of grass and water / and as a poor man loves a loaf of bread!"[23] Pledging that they will remain companions forever, the poet invites his beloved to journey beside him, hand in hand, for eternity, without questioning where fate might lead them. In the poem "My Beloved Rises from Her Sleep," the land is depicted as "a composite of all the women of the pure tongue" whose exceptional beauty dazzles her lover: "I remain lost in her body / The smell of earth that never perishes."[24] Grieving over her downfall, the poet is speechless with sorrow: "For every occasion there is a saying, / But your death took speech unawares / And was a reward for exiles / and a prize for darkness."[25] In the poem "A Lover from Palestine," the land is alternately depicted as a shepherdess without a flock who is fleeing from her pursuers, as a romantic figure among desolate ruins (alluding to the abandoned desert campsite of the idolized beloved in the odes of pre-Islamic Arabia), and as a garden belonging to the lover, who is knocking at the door of his own heart. The denied lover desperately seeks to be united with his beloved: "Take me as a relic from the mansion of sorrow; / Take me as a verse from my tragedy; / Take me as a toy, a brick from the house / So that our children will remember to return."[26] Such passionate love poems for the land transcend the conventions of both patriotic poetry and traditional love poetry.

Over the years, the role of "a lover from Palestine" became Darwish's most consistent public persona.[27] In "Reading My Beloved's Face," the poet gazes at his beloved's eyes and sees his nation's history: lost cities, a crimson time (i.e., bloodshed), utopia, and childhood. Adding that he sees in her eyes the reason for death and pride, he says: "My country is nothing but these eyes / that turn the land into a body."[28] Within the fertile female body of the beloved lies the potential for the nation's rebirth. Yet, despite the lover's loyalty and devotion, the beloved does not return his love. In the poem "I Am the Unlucky Lover," the poet bemoans his bad luck in being the object of unrequited love. In poignant lines, he protests: "I love, I love, I love you. But I do not want to travel on your wave. / Let me be, leave me, as the sea leaves its shells / On the eternal coast of exile. / I am the unlucky lover. I cannot come to you. And I cannot return to myself."[29]

Such ardent love poems for the homeland had tremendous political, cultural, and emotional significance for the Palestinians: they nourished their sense of national pride, asserted their strong attachment to the land, and voiced their pain and suffering for being separated from it. Darwish became the poet of resistance par excellence; his audience had a great demand for these poems, and he was expected to satisfy this demand. Every love poem that he wrote, whether it was from a son to his mother, expressing his yearning for her coffee and bread (e.g., the famous poem "To My Mother"[30]), or as a man to a woman (e.g., "Longing for the Light"[31]), was interpreted as a love poem for the homeland. This situation put pressure on Darwish's poetic sensibilities. As he began to mature as a poet, he found himself trapped by the taste and expectations of his audience. When he left Israel in 1970 and went into a self-imposed exile, it was not only because he wanted to escape political persecution by the Israeli authorities, but also because he aspired for professional growth as a poet, for a change in his writing—both in style and theme—and for the freedom to express his individuality and independence. Focusing exclusively on the cause of Palestine was constricting his range of creativity: "I wanted to develop, to fly in the open space," he said, as he explained the various reasons for his departure, an act that was criticized by Palestinians and across the Arab world as abandonment of his people.[32]

The Syrian scholar Munir Akash describes the tensions that existed between the public's taste and Darwish's desire for aesthetic control over his poetry: "Ever since I first came to know Mahmoud Darwish, I have watched him bear the brunt of his audience's zeal. Unlike other Palestinian poets of his generation, he has been lauded as a hero, magnified into a myth and made the official national poet of Palestine. His people love him. They chant his odes in their fields, in their schools, on their marches and in their miserable tin shanty-towns. But many of his admirers think they possess him, often disregarding the poetical aspect of his humane nature, judging him harshly when he succumbs to human emotions, such as feeling sad or weak or happy, being unpoetically grumpy or, unthinkably, writing love poems instead of poems of political outrage."[33] Akash cites the Lebanese poet Yusuf al-Khal as having said that "the best way for Mahmoud Darwish to become a great poet was for him to resist any compromise with the taste of his audience."[34]

Following his departure from Israel in 1970, Darwish spent a year of study in Moscow, where he was sent by Rakah, the Israeli Communist Party. In 1971 he arrived in Cairo, where he stayed for about a year, working at *al-Ahram* daily newspaper in the company of great Egyptian writers such as Naguib Mahfouz, Tawfiq al-Hakim, and Yusuf Idris. In 1972 he moved to Beirut, where he joined the Palestine Liberation Organization (PLO) and became one of its central activists, editing the PLO Research

Center's journal *Shu'un Filastiniyya* (Palestinian Affairs). He stayed in Beirut a decade (1972–1982) during which he produced prolific poetry marked by a mix of the political/collective and the personal/individual, until he had to leave this city too, when Israel and its Lebanese Christian (Maronite) allies succeeded in expelling the PLO from the country. After a short stay in Tunisia, he left for Paris, where he spent a relatively long period (1983–1995) and wrote the best of his poetry, with an increasing emphasis on the personal, as exemplified by the collections *Fewer Roses* (1986), *Eleven Planets* (1992), and *Why Did You Leave the Horse Alone?* (1995). Following the signing of the Oslo Accords between the Israeli government and the leadership of the PLO in 1993, Darwish's exile ended. Carrying a Palestinian identity card, he arrived in Israel for a three-day visit. In 1996 he returned to the land, dividing his time between Amman, Jordan, and Ramallah, the de facto Palestinian capital on the West Bank. Devoting himself to literature, he worked as director of the Palestine Literary Institute and as editor-in-chief of its journal, *al-Karmel*. He continued to write lyrical poetry, with bold historical allegories of the Palestinian experience and a reliance on myth and metaphysics, and to foster all aspects of Palestinian culture and heritage. He died on 9 August 2008, at the age of sixty-seven, following heart surgery in Houston, Texas, and was given a state funeral in Ramallah, where he was laid to rest.

When Darwish's collection *A Bed for the Stranger*—his first volume of poems devoted entirely to love—came out in 1999, his readers were shocked by what many saw as his abandonment of the cause of Palestine and retreat into selfish concerns.[35] If Darwish's readers judged him critically when he wrote love poems instead of poems with national/political content, one can only imagine what their reactions would have been if they had known that some of his earlier love poems were dedicated to an Israeli-Jewish woman. No wonder, then, that Darwish refrained from referring to her by her real name and instead used the pseudonym Rita. The "Rita" poems appear as early as 1967, in his collection *The End of the Night*, and as late as 1992, in his collection *Eleven Planets*. In addition, he devoted passages to her in his prose works *Journal of an Ordinary Grief* (1973) and *Memory for Forgetfulness* (1986).

The criticism with which Darwish's love poems were received by many among his audience raises the intriguing question of what the poet's obligations are toward his readers, who demand to be given topics of interest to them. "Does Mahmoud Darwish have a right to produce a book of poetry solely dedicated to love?" asks the Syrian scholar Subhi Hadidi in his essay on Darwish's love poems. "He is considered the 'poet of resistance,' 'the conscience of Palestine,' 'the lover of the land,' as Arabic literary criticism has so often represented him and confined him."[36] Hadidi concedes that while it may seem self-evident that Darwish should be allowed to love as others do and to write a love poem for a woman—a beloved who is of flesh and blood and not only a metaphor for Palestine or the land or the cause—in reality, the matter is much more complicated. He points out that circumstances, both objective and subjective, have led Darwish to occupy a position of significance similar to that of the great poets of the Arab past. The adulation of the public put pressures on him, forbidding him from walking away from his collective duties and the functions that have been assigned to him as the voice of his people. When Darwish left Israel in 1970 and began to gain greater literary authority, he became keenly aware of the problematic position of the poet who is made into a spokesman for the collective. In order not to lose aesthetic control of his poetry, he had to establish a certain balance between his poetic quest and public expectations. On the one hand, he insisted that his voice must remain different from that of the public and did not hesitate to distance himself from the public when it asked for political responses. On the other hand, he was forced to innovate, to constantly rethink the material and topics of his poetry. In Hadidi's view, by refusing to surrender to ideology and populism, Darwish managed to protect the integrity of his poetry and also to renew it constantly.[37]

Darwish defended *A Bed for the Stranger*—his first volume of poems devoted entirely to love—by arguing that even the ability to love is a form of resistance: "We Palestinians are supposed to be dedicated to one subject—liberating Palestine. This is a prison. We're human, we love, we fear death, we enjoy the first flowers of spring. So, to express this is resistance against having our subject dictated to us. If I write love poems, I resist the conditions that don't allow me to write love poems."[38] The tension between the private lyrical mode and the public declamatory one persisted in Darwish's poetic work, and his public persona continued to be in marked contrast to his private life. The Palestinian poet Fady Joudah describes him as "a very shy, shy man who was—who people flocked to, and he also was a very gentle and generous man who knew a lot of them wanted so much from him—a cup of coffee, a conversation, a signature. He cherished his private life a lot, because he also knew that his—most of his other life was public. In his great poem 'Mural,' he ends it with a line: 'I am not mine, I am not mine, I am not mine.'"[39] Darwish's keen insight into his own life

10 D. COHEN-MOR

and destiny explains to a great extent why his love affair with "Rita" was largely shrouded in silence and mystery.[40]

NOTES

1. "The Hoopoe," in Mahmoud Darwish, *Unfortunately, It Was Paradise: Selected Poems*, trans. and ed. Munir Akash and Carolyn Forche (with Sinan Antoon and Amira El-Zein) (Berkeley: University of California Press, 2003), p. 31. For the Arabic text, see "Al-Hudhud," in Mahmoud Darwish, *Al-Diwan: al-a'mal al-ula* (3 vols. Beirut: Riad El-Rayyes, 2005), 3: 249.
2. Mahmoud Darwish, "Diary of Palestinian Wound," trans. Lena Jayyusi and Christopher Middleton, in *Modern Arabic Poetry: An Anthology*, ed. Salma Khadra Jayyusi (New York: Columbia University Press, 1987), p. 202. For the Arabic text, see "Yawmiyyat jurh Filastini," in Darwish, *Al-Diwan: al-a'mal al-ula*, 1: 361.
3. Robyn Creswell, "Unbeliever in the Impossible: The Poetry of Mahmoud Darwish," *Harper's Magazine* (February 2009), pp. 69–74. http://search.proquest.com. Accessed 21 December 2016. Cited from the online version, p. 4.
4. "A Lover from Palestine" ("'Ashiq min Filastin") appears in Darwish, *Al-Diwan: al-a'mal al-ula*, 1: 87–94; translated by Badreddine M. Bennani, *Journal of Arabic Literature* 5 (1974): 129–133. Cited from p. 129.
5. Ibid., p. 132.
6. Ibid.
7. Khaled Mattawa, *Mahmoud Darwish: The Poet's Art and His Nation* (Syracuse: Syracuse University Press, 2014), p. 50.
8. Cited from the poem "Nashid ma" ("A Certain Hymn") in Darwish, *Al-Diwan: al-a'mal al-ula*, p. 18. Translation mine.
9. Ibid., p. 19. Translation mine.
10. Cited from the poem "I Am the Unlucky Lover," in Mahmoud Darwish, *I Don't Want This Poem to End: Early and Late Poems*, ed. and trans. Mohammad Shaheen (Northampton: Interlink Books, 2017), p. 99. For the Arabic text, see "Ana al-'ashiq al-sayy' al-hazz," in Darwish, *Al-Diwan: al-a'mal al-ula*, 3: 49–53.
11. "To My Mother" ("Ila ummi") first appeared in Darwish's collection *'Ashiq min Filastin*, 1966; reprinted in Darwish, *Al-Diwan: al-a'mal al-ula*, 1: 106–107. For a translation, see *Selected Poems: Mahmoud Darwish*, introduced and translated by Ian Wedde and Fawwaz Tuqan (Cheadle Hulme, UK: Carcanet, 1973), p. 66.
12. The present account of Darwish's life is based on Muna Abu Eid, *Mahmoud Darwish: Literature and the Politics of Palestinian Identity* (London: I. B. Taurus, 2016), pp. 15–48; and Reuven Snir, *Mahmoud Darwish: hamishim shnot shira* (Fifty Years of Poetry) (Tel Aviv: Keshev, 2015), pp. 17–58.

1 THE POET'S PUBLIC PERSONA: A LOVER FROM PALESTINE   11

13. Abu Eid, *Mahmoud Darwish*, p. 16.
14. These poems are included in Mahmoud Darwish, *Why Did You Leave the Horse Alone*, trans. Jeffery Sacks (Brooklyn: Archipelago, 2006), pp. 22–27 and 36–40, respectively.
15. *Al-Karmel* 86 (Winter 2006): 29–30. Cited in Snir, *Mahmoud Darwish: hamishim shnot shira*, p. 5. Translation mine.
16. Abu Eid, *Mahmoud Darwish*, p. 30.
17. "Identity Card," trans. Wedde and Tuqan, in *Selected Poems: Mahmoud Darwish*, pp. 24–25. For the Arabic text, see "Bitaqat huwiyya," in Darwish, *Al-Diwan: al-a'mal al-ula*, 1: 80–84.
18. For additional information on the use of the term Palestinian vs. Arab, see "'Write down I Am an Arab': Scholars Q & A on 2014 Mahmoud Darwish Documentary," posted on 14 September 2015 on tirnscholars.org.
19. Mahmoud Darwish, *Memory for Forgetfulness: August, Beirut, 1982*, trans. Ibrahim Muhawi (Berkeley: University of California Press, 1995), p. 174.
20. Creswell, "Unbeliever in the Impossible," p. 4.
21. *Al-Dawliya* (13 May 1991), p. 31. Cited in Snir, *Mahmoud Darwish: hamishim shnot shira*, p. 76. Translation mine.
22. Creswell, "Unbeliever in the Impossible," p. 5.
23. "The Most Beautiful Love" ("Ajmal hubb") first appeared in Darwish's collection *Olive Leaves*, 1964; reprinted in Darwish, *Al-Diwan: al-a'mal al-ula*, pp. 69–70. Translation mine.
24. "My Beloved Rises from Her Sleep" ("Habibati tanhad min nawmiha") appears in Darwish, *Al-Diwan: al-a'mal al-ula*, 1: 325–337; translated by B. M. Bennani, *Journal of Arabic Literature* 6 (1975): 101–106. Cited from p. 102.
25. Ibid., p. 103.
26. "A Lover from Palestine" ("'Ashiq min Filastin") appears in Darwish, *Al-Diwan: al-a'mal al-ula*, 1: 92–93; translated by Badreddine M. Bennani, *Journal of Arabic Literature* 5 (1974): 132.
27. Mattawa, *Mahmoud Darwish*, p. 46.
28. Cited from ibid., p. 48. For the Arabic text, see "Qira'a fi wajh habibati," in Darwish, *Al-Diwan: al-a'mal al-ula*, 1: 310.
29. "I Am the Unlucky Lover," trans. Shaheen, in *Mahmoud Darwish, I Don't Want This Poem to End*, p. 101. For the Arabic text, see Darwish "Ana al-'ashiq al-sayy' al-hazz," in *Al-Diwan: al-a'mal al-ula*, 3: 49–53.
30. "To My Mother," trans. Wedde and Tuqan, in *Selected Poems: Mahmoud Darwish*, p. 66; for the Arabic text, see "Ila ummi," in Darwish, *Al-Diwan: al-a'mal al-ula*, 1: 106–107.
31. "Longing for the Light," trans. Wedde and Tuqan, in *Selected Poems: Mahmoud Darwish*, p. 36; for the Arabic text, see "Hanin ila al-daw'," in Darwish, *Al-Diwan: al-a'mal al-ula*, 1: 78–79.
32. Abu Eid, *Mahmoud Darwish*, p. 34.

33. Munir Akash, in the introduction to *Mahmoud Darwish: The Adam of Two Edens: Poems*, ed. Munir Akash and Daniel Moore (Syracuse: Syracuse University Press, 2000), p. 19.
34. Ibid., p. 22.
35. Ibid., p. 19.
36. Subhi Hadidi, "Mahmoud Darwish's Love Poem: History, Exile, and the Epic Call," in *Mahmoud Darwish, Exile's Poet: Critical Essays*, ed. Hala Khamis Nassar and Najat Rahman (Northampton: Olive Branch Press, 2008), p. 95.
37. Ibid., pp. 97–98.
38. Maya Jaggi, "Poet of the Arab World: Mahmoud Darwish." *The Guardian* (7 June 2002), p. 8. https://theguardian.com/books. Accessed 16 August 2016.
39. Cited from Amy Goodman, "Mahmoud Darwish, Poet Laureate of the Palestinians, 1941–2008," *Democracy Now* (11 August 2008), p. 2. www.democracynow.org. Accessed 14 November 2016.
40. Although some Arab scholars like Abdullah al-Shahham (1988) and Kamal Abdel-Malek (2005) have acknowledged that Rita refers to an Israeli-Jewish woman, they could not identify her by name, could not provide an account of her life and career, and could not chronicle Darwish's relationship with her. See the bibliography for these scholars' studies.

CHAPTER 2

Dangerous Liaisons: Arab-Jewish Romantic Relationships

Abstract This chapter provides background information on interfaith dating and marriage in Israel to contextualize the complications surrounding Darwish's love affair with Rita. I look at the prevailing social attitudes toward this issue, the existing laws, and the statistics on both sides of the ethno-religious divide. Regarded as an act of treason by members of both Arab and Jewish societies, interfaith romance and marriage are discouraged and incur great hardships for couples who violate this taboo. The situation on the ground is mirrored in works of fiction by both Arab and Jewish authors in Israel, and I present many examples of novels and short stories that depict such relationships, almost all of which end in heartache, breakup, or death.

Keywords Love across ethno-religious divide—social taboo · Arab-Jewish intimate relationships—social attitudes—Israel · Arab-Jewish romance—depictions—Hebrew fiction · Arab-Jewish romance—depictions—Arabic fiction

Love across ethno-religious lines is a taboo in many societies, especially when the relations between the different ethno-religious groups are

© The Author(s) 2019
D. Cohen-Mor, *Mahmoud Darwish*,
https://doi.org/10.1007/978-3-030-24162-9_2

13

marked by hostility. History abounds with tragic stories of lovers caught in the middle of the conflict between their respective communities. Recent examples include the thirty-year-period of Troubles in Northern Ireland (1968–1998), as the sectarian strife there came to be known, when Catholic Irish girls accused of having intimate relationships with British soldiers were subjected to a popular form of punishment called "tarring and feathering" by members of the Irish Republican Army. These girls had their heads shaved before being dragged to a lamppost, where they were tied up and had hot tar poured over their heads, followed by the dumping of feathers, which would stick to the tar for days, acting as a reminder of their "crimes" against their community. This kind of punishment, designed to publicly humiliate and degrade the victim, dates back to the Crusades, when it was used to enforce informal justice throughout Europe and its colonies. Similarly, during the fifteen-year-long sectarian war between Muslim and Christian Arabs in Lebanon (1975–1990), lovers from opposing camps suffered severe retribution and were even abducted and put to death by armed militiamen, as is poignantly depicted in the novel *Sitt Marie Rose* by the Lebanese author Etel Adnan.[1]

Israel is no exception to the prevailing taboo on romance and marriage across ethno-religious lines. Arabs make up a fifth of Israel's population, but intimate relationships between Arabs and Jews are rare. Opposition to such relationships is shared by the vast majority of Israeli-Jews, who regard this issue as a threat to the state's Jewishness. One of the few surveys of the subject conducted by the Tel Aviv Geocartography Institute in 2007 found that over half the Jewish population in Israel believes that the marriage of a Jewish woman to an Arab man is equal to "national treason."[2] Another survey conducted by *Haaretz* newspaper and the Dialog company in 2014 found that nearly three-quarters of Israeli-Jews and two-thirds of Israeli-Arabs would not marry someone from a different religion. Among Muslim Israeli-Arabs, seventy-one percent opposed interfaith relationships, whereas among Christian Israeli-Arabs fifty percent were opposed.[3] Furthermore, the survey found that across religious denominations, Israeli-Jews would be much more opposed to their relatives marrying Arabs than they would be to relatives marrying other non-Jews. Only a third of secular Jewish-Israelis would be opposed to a relative marrying an American or European Christian, but a majority would oppose a relative marrying an Arab. Opposition to intermarriage was lowest among immigrants from the former Soviet Union, presumably because they did not undergo the religious and Zionist education that more established Israeli-Jews received.[4]

Since the establishment of the State of Israel in 1948, a number of legal and administrative measures have been taken to limit the possibilities of close relations developing between Jewish and Arab citizens. Largely segregated communities and separate education systems mean that there are few opportunities for young Arab and Jews to interact and get to know each other. Even in the few "mixed cities," Arab residents are usually confined to separate neighborhoods. All personal status issues in each community are under the jurisdiction of their own religious authorities. Marriages across religious lines are prohibited by law: Jews may not marry Christians; Muslims may not marry Jews; Christians may not marry Muslims. Civil marriage is banned in Israel, which means that in the small number of cases where a Jew and an Arab want to marry each other, they must either do so by leaving the country to wed abroad (the marriage is recognized upon the couple's return), or one of them must convert to the other's religion, in which case their marriage is registered as if it were between Muslim and Muslim, or Jew and Jew, or Christian and Christian.[5] The sociologist Yuval Yonay states that the Central Bureau of Statistics does not deal with interfaith marriages simply because their number is too small to be studied: "Separation between Jews and Arabs is so ingrained in Israeli society, it is surprising that anyone manages to escape these central controls."[6] Sammy Smooha, a specialist in comparative ethnic relations, asserts that Israel knows of no more than a thousand instances in which a Jew married an Arab since the creation of the state. "Even if there is any information on the matter," he remarks, "I doubt it's going to be published, firstly because the phenomenon would spark a lot of opposition among religious circles, fearing that the revelation of such data would encourage other people to leave their faith. And, secondly, because any such case is considered a 'failure' by the society that didn't do enough to keep people inside Judaism."[7]

Although the Hebrew Bible contains several positive examples of mixed marriages—such as that of Moses, who married Tziporah, the daughter of a Midianite priest, and that of queen Esther, who married the Persian king Ahashverosh—it does not look favorably on interfaith marriages, warning that "your children will turn away from Me to worship other gods" (Deuteronomy 7: 1–3). Smooha points out that in Israel "both Jews and Arabs oppose interfaith unions, clinging to their culture, traditions, and Zionist/Palestinian ideology. So the refusal to marry a person from another faith is not perceived as racism, but rather as a *cultural norm*."[8] The mixed marriages that do take place usually involve a Jewish woman and a Muslim man. The women often come from low socioeconomic backgrounds and are escaping problems at home, or are immigrants from the former Soviet Union who are more accepting of such unions. Most of these couples choose to reside in an Arab village to avoid being rejected by the Jewish majority of the country. But even if the woman manages to adjust to the customs and values of an Arab village, the couple still faces a major challenge regarding the upbringing of their children. Should they raise them as Muslims or as Jews? The issue of identity is crucial: according to Jewish law, when the mother is Jewish the child is considered Jewish, and thus he would have to serve in the army; but, given that the child is raised in Arab society, it is questionable whether he would be faithful to the State of Israel.[9]

While Judaism is matrilineal, Islam is patrilineal. According to Muslim law, children born to a Muslim man married to a Jewish woman are considered Muslim. When such a marriage falls apart, the issue of child custody can lead to a tug of war between the Jewish and Muslim religious authorities, both of which lay claim to the identity of the child. As for interfaith marriage, the Koran (5: 5 and 2: 221) provides clear guidelines on the topic: it is lawful if the husband is Muslim and the wife is from among the "people of the book" (i.e., the Holy Scripture), namely, Jews or Christians; polytheists and idolaters are forbidden. The Muslim woman, however, is not allowed to marry a man of another faith, unless he converts to Islam. This prohibition is closely related to the patrilineal aspect of Islam and its mission to populate the world with believers. Hence marriages between Muslim-Arab women and Israeli-Jewish men are extremely rare.

Several local authorities in Israel have undertaken measures to prevent Jewish–Arab intermarriage. The municipality of Petah Tikva, for example, a city (6.5 mi) east of Tel Aviv, announced in 2009 that it was establishing a special team of youth counselors and psychologists whose job is to identify young Jewish women who are dating Arab men and "rescue" them. Petah Tikva's hostility to Arab men mixing with local Jewish women is shared by other Israeli communities. Residents of Pisgat Zeev, a large Jewish settlement in the midst of Palestinian neighborhoods in East Jerusalem, have formed a vigilante-style patrol called "Fire for Judaism" to stop interfaith dating. In 2008, the municipality of Kiryat Gat, a town in southern Israel, launched a program in schools to warn Jewish girls of the dangers of dating Bedouin men. The girls were shown a video titled "Sleeping with the Enemy," which described mixed couples as an "unnatural phenomenon." Similarly, the northern town of Safed hung up posters all over its territory warning Jewish women of the dangers of dating Arab men, an experience that would only lead to beatings, hard drugs, prostitution, and crime. Safed's chief rabbi, Shmuel Eliyahu, told a local newspaper that seducing Jewish girls was another form of "warfare" by Arab men. Both the campaigns of Kiryat Gat and Safed were supported by an orthodox organization called Yad L'Achim (A Helping Hand for Brothers), which runs an anti-assimilation program publicly dedicated to protecting Jewish girls from interfaith relationships and preventing them from dating and marrying Arab men. Their members view Arab-Jewish marriages as part of the larger Arab-Israeli conflict and interpret them as acts of revenge by the Arabs, who seek to wipe out the Jewish people this way.[10]

The journalist David Shipler, who interviewed several Arab-Jewish couples in Israel, describes their predicament in detail: "Practically everyone who enters into a mixed Arab-Jewish marriage faces some hardship, usually estrangement from society or family, sometimes a clash of styles and expectations in the home as the two cultures attempt to mesh." The crux of the problem is that "no middle ground exists in Israel between Arab and Jewish societies, and so the couple must choose to live on one side of the divide or the other." The weight of the surrounding strife does not allow the union to experience the natural ease of loving: "Never can it soar, carefree. Always it must be an act of conviction, defiance, a statement of belief in the purity of the person above the society's neat grid of religious and ethnic definitions." Not surprisingly, in the homes of mixed Arab-Jewish couples one can hear the finest statements of tolerance: "A human being is not an Arab or a Jew but a human being."[11] A documentary film titled *Forbidden Marriages in the Holy Land*, by the Palestinian director Michel Khleifi (1995), explores the lives and loves of eight mixed Arab-Jewish couples from different generations and backgrounds, detailing the struggles they face to balance their relationship with their familial, cultural, religious, national, and political ties, highlighting complex issues such as identity and belonging, and exposing the mutual intolerance of Christianity, Islam, and Judaism.

The prevailing social attitudes toward intimate relationships between Arabs and Jews in Israel are mirrored in both Arabic and Hebrew works of literature. Comparatively speaking, there is a paucity of works dealing with this sensitive topic in Arabic fiction, a fact that indicates that this type of relations is a taboo subject. This becomes all the more obvious when one considers the abundance of Arabic works of fiction that deal with romantic relationships across other ethno-religious lines, such as between Arabs and Westerners, or between Christian Arabs and Muslim Arabs. Yusuf Idris's poignant story "Egyptian Mona Lisa," for example, depicts the unrequited love of a Muslim boy for a Coptic girl in a small village community in Egypt,[12] and his novella *The Sinners* has as a subplot the eloping of a Coptic woman who resides on a cotton estate in the Nile delta with a Muslim man employed as a clerk there.[13] Suleiman Fayyad's novel *Voices* portrays the theme of East–West encounter through the fate of a mixed Egyptian-French couple who comes from France for a visit in the husband's home village. The village women, gripped by envy and fear of the foreign woman's exuberant sexuality, attack her when she is alone and forcibly circumcise her, a brutal act that results in her bleeding to death.[14] Most Arabic coming-of-age novels (so-called bildungsroman) feature a journey of the male protagonist to the West, where he has various adventures, including a love affair with a European or an American woman, as part of his self-development and passage into adulthood. Some pertinent examples are Yahya Haqqi's *The Saint's Lamp* (1944), Suhayl Idris's *The Latin Quarter* (1953), Tayyib Saleh's *Season of Migration to the North* (1969), Ghalib Hamza Abu al-Faraj's *The Lost Years* (1980), and Ezzedine Choukri Fishere's *Embrace on Brooklyn Bridge* (2011).[15] In all of these works, the experience of romantic love across ethno-religious lines, though frequently painful, contributes to the hero's growth and initiation into life. It is striking that leading Arab fiction writers such as the Egyptian Naguib Mahfouz and Yusuf Idris, the Syrian Zakaria Tamer, the Lebanese Rashid al-Daif, and the Moroccan Mohamed Choukri (to mention but a few) have dared writing on sensitive topics such as homosexuality, premarital sex, politics, and religion, but have avoided the topic of romantic love between Arabs and Jews altogether.

As for Arab women writers, much like their male counterparts, their coming-of-age novels are often structured around the heroine's journey abroad, where she undergoes a variety of experiences, among them a love affair with a European or an American man, all of which exposes her to opposed cultural values and worldviews and promotes her acquisition of self-knowledge.[16] However, unlike the Arabic male bildungsroman, which generally ends on a positive note with the hero's return to his home country ready to assume his place in society and fulfill his destiny, the Arabic female bildungsroman often ends on a tragic note. In Somaya Ramadan's *Leaves of Narcissus* (2001),[17] for example, the heroine, a young Egyptian woman who goes to Dublin, Ireland, in search of higher education, is unable to cope with the profound sense of alienation and identity crisis that this East–West encounter, including a romantic relationship with a colleague, creates in her; she suffers a severe mental breakdown that results in her withdrawal from reality and from society. Ramziya Abbas al-Iryani's novella *The Stranger* (1999) tells of the forbidden love of a Yemeni girl from a conservative Muslim family for an American man whom she meets in the United States, where her father has taken her in his pursuit of postgraduate studies. Strongly opposed to this relationship, the father decides to send his daughter back to Yemen and marry her off to her cousin, thereby driving her to a mental breakdown that precipitates her untimely death.[18] In Miral al-Tahawy's *Brooklyn Heights* (2010),[19] an autobiographical novel of displacement and self-discovery, an Egyptian single mother, Hend, moves with her little son to New York after the breakup of her marriage, hoping for a new beginning. She lives in an ethnically diverse community in Brooklyn, where she meets other immigrants who dream of change, love, and self-fulfillment, and shares in their experiences. Feeling lonely and adrift, she takes tango lessons from an American dance instructor in her apartment building and dates him a couple of times, but when she rebuffs his sexual advances he quickly moves on to one of her friends, who spends nights with him. Bewildered by her new world and haunted by memories from her past, Hend sinks into a prolonged depression that cripples her ability to function. As is the case with their male counterparts, Arab women writers generally refrain from depicting romantic relationships between Arabs and Jews in their literary works. It is striking that the Lebanese author Hanan al-Shaykh, for example, who is known for her daring exploration of female sexuality in her writings, and whose novels often depict unconventional love stories of Arab women both within and across ethno-religious lines (e.g., *The Story of Zahra*, *Women of Sand and Myrrh*, and *Only in London*), has never portrayed romantic love between Arabs and Jews.

Given the centrality of the Arab-Israeli conflict in the modern history of the Middle East, it is perhaps not surprising that Arabic works of fiction that feature Jewish characters generally equate them with Zionists and portray them in highly negative terms that preclude any possibility of romantic relationships. Frequently, such works are an extension of purely political polemics, aimed at dehumanizing the enemy and justifying the continuation of the war against them until victory is finally achieved. A classic example is the novella *Far from Land* (1961) by the Egyptian writer Ihsan Abd al-Quddus.[20] Set in 1948, the story tells of a shipboard romance between Hasan, an Egyptian journalist dedicated to the Palestinian cause, and Maria, an American-Jewish woman living in Mandatory Palestine. On a voyage to the United States, they fall in love and spend blissful days together, until they receive news that war has broken out in Palestine. The passage

20   D. COHEN-MOR

in which Hasan first becomes aware that Maria (an unusual name choice for a Jewish girl) is Jewish reads like a polemical piece that is intended to contrast Arab tolerance with Zionist fanaticism:

> "I'm Jewish," she announced.

> I simply stood there dumbfounded. So what if she was Jewish? There were three Jews among my colleagues at work; one was an artist, one worked in the advertising department and the third in accounting. And I had plenty of Jewish friends in Cairo. When I had lived in Abbasiyya ten years before, I had fallen in love with a girl from the Jewish quarter of al-Zahir.

> "And I'm a Muslim; but so what?" I said at last, trying to calm her.

> She spoke out again, quiet but vehement as before:

> "You don't understand. You don't want to emerge from your childhood innocence. I'm Jewish and I live in Palestine. And more than that; I'm enrolled in the Haganah forces. Do you know what that means? That we're enemies, that it's my duty now to spy on you, to pry from you all the information you have. You've already given me a lot. And I've done the same with many Arabs I've met in Jerusalem, Jaffa, and Beirut. But now I'm on vacation. I don't want to work; I want to forget Haganah, forget Palestine. I want to have some rest. Can you understand? I want to relax but I can never do that with you. With you I must fight." (pp. 236–237)

Filled with sympathy for Maria, Hasan realizes that a great barrier has risen between them and that to attain her he must destroy it. This barrier—Zionism—is not merely a plan to gain control over a piece of land, but a threat to humanity: "Zionism was … a call for the very destruction of mankind, for the destruction of love, of beauty and of peace. It instilled a poison into people's hearts, transforming them into dry chunks of rancor and hatred. I could feel the poison working on myself. … I had a sudden urge to kill, to murder all the Zionists. For the first time I began thinking of taking part in the battle, not with my pen but with weapons" (p. 237).

Regarding Maria as a victim who needs protection from her own people, he tries to reason with her that she is confused and that she will be fighting on the side of violence and greed, but to no avail. For the remainder of their days at sea, they try to forget their irreconcilable positions over Palestine and construct for themselves a world of love and harmony, but they fail. Each convinced that the other is misguided by an unjust ideology, they argue repeatedly about the question of whose homeland Palestine rightfully is. At one point, Maria expresses a wish to remain at sea, "far from land" (hence the novella's title) and thus free from strife: "If only we had a wooden raft where we could live amidst the ocean. Then we could live in peace." Agreeing, Hasan replies, "Then we'd not argue. We'd be neither Jew nor Muslim, American nor Arab. We'd be just two of God's creations" (p. 245).

As neither of them is able to win the other over to the opposite point of view, they gloomily accept that each will fight for their own cause, even if this means that one lover might actually kill the other on the battlefield. When the ship arrives at its destination, they go their separate ways. Hasan becomes a warrior, fighting for the cause of Palestine and against Zionism, "revolting on behalf of both the Arabs and the Jews" (p. 248), knowing he "could never love again until Palestine was freed" (p. 249). Five years later, he travels to New York City on official business and, going into a department store on Fifth Avenue, he runs into Maria. Astonished to meet her there looking serene and contented, he has a brief exchange with her:

> "When did you come to New York?" I asked at last.
> "Oh, I live here," she replied, smiling.
> "Since when?" I inquired, very surprised.
> "For the past five years," she stated, not looking directly at me.
> "And what about Israel?"
> "Oh, I'm an American," she said simply, smiling.
> "And Israel?"
> "I left it," she said, looking down at her shoes.
> "Why?" I asked, my astonishment growing.
> "Perhaps, because I could never kill you!" she said, smiling slightly and looking up to my eyes. (p. 249)

The story ends on a triumphant note for Hasan: although the military battle for Palestine was lost, the moral battle was won. Maria has abandoned Zionism and accepted cross-cultural and humanistic values. As she walks away, he stares after her, but now he has "real hope, hope for the future of man" (p. 249). A politically loaded story, it reduces the complex question of Arab-Jewish romantic relationships to one dimension—the ideological.

An earlier work of fiction titled *The Heir* (*Al-Warith*, 1920), by the Palestinian Khalil Baydas,[21] merits mention because the author is regarded as the father of Palestinian fiction. The novel offers an unsubtle account of a love affair between Aziz, the son of a Syrian merchant family that has emigrated to Egypt, and Esther, a Jewish dancer whom he meets there.

22   D. COHEN-MOR

Esther is portrayed as a promiscuous and unscrupulous woman who seeks to extort money from Aziz with the help of other Jews in her group. The unsuspecting Aziz falls into her trap and incurs heavy debts that bring him to the brink of bankruptcy and nervous breakdown, but he is ultimately saved by returning to the family fold and marrying his cousin. The novel does not treat any of the problems encountered in an intimate relationship between an Arab and a Jew; instead, it merely presents a pejorative, stereotyped portrait of Jews as insatiably greedy, corrupt, and deceitful.

More recently, Alaa Al Aswany's *Chicago* (2007),[22] a political novel depicting the Egyptian experience in post-9/11 America, has as one of its many subplots a love affair between Nagi Abd al-Samad, an Egyptian medical student at the University of Illinois, and Wendy Shore, a Jewish stockbroker at the Chicago Stock exchange. Nagi, a dissident poet banned from Cairo's university system, seeks a safe haven in science. Almost from the start, he is shown to be obsessed with sex: on the first day of his arrival on the university campus, he searches for sexual services on the internet and hires a prostitute to come to his apartment. Expecting her to be a young buxom blonde, he is disgusted when she turns out to be a fat middle-aged black woman and promptly kicks her out. Thus, it comes as no surprise when he falls for Wendy, a young, blonde, blue-eyed, and fair-skinned woman whom he meets in a bar. When she reveals to him that she is Jewish and asks if he is shocked, he replies with a polemical argument: "The Arabs hate Israel not because it is a state for the Jews but because it stole Palestine and committed dozens of massacres against the Palestinians. If the Israelis were Hindus or Buddhists, it wouldn't have changed anything for us. Our conflict with Israel is political and not religious" (p. 208). Then he launches into a lofty speech about how Jews lived under Arab rule for many centuries without problems or persecution, distorting historical facts and painting an embellished picture of Arab tolerance and complete trust in the Jewish other. When news of their romantic relationship spreads at the university, Nagi experiences harassment from a number of fanatic Jewish students but chooses to ignore it in a demonstration of tolerance. However, the real test of his lofty speech about Arab tolerance and trust in the Jewish other comes when one day he returns to his apartment and finds that a sleazy agent from the Egyptian Embassy in Washington has invaded it, warning him to cease his dissident political activities and informing him that he knows about his relationship with Wendy and even has videos of the two of them having sex. Nagi immediately suspects that Wendy is the person who provided this information to the agent and also gave him a copy of his apartment key. When he confronts her with his suspicion, she realizes that their relationship has no future and decides to end it. "Our fight brought the truth to the open," she tells him. "Ultimately, I belong to the enemies of your country. No matter how much you love me, you'll never forget that I'm Jewish. No matter how faithful I remain to you, your trust in me will always be fragile. I'll be the first suspect in your view" (pp. 301–302). Once again, the Arab-Jewish romance fails, leaving both characters with a heartache. Although in this novel Al Aswany lives up to his reputation for breaking social taboos, his portrayal of the Arab-Jewish romance lacks both depth and verisimilitude. For one thing, Nagi treats Wendy like a sexual plaything rather than a beloved, and sex for him is primarily an act of satisfying his erotic needs rather than an act of connection and intimacy. For another, Wendy is a thinly drawn character who merely represents an opposing point of view. The narrative's message seems to be that an Arab-Jewish romance is untenable *even when* it takes place far away from the conflicted Middle East in an open and free country like the United States.

The Egyptian literary scholar Kamal Abdel-Malek, known for his keen interest in cultural encounters between Arabs and Jews, has recently self-published a novel in the English language titled *Come with Me from Jerusalem* (2013).[23] Set in the aftermath of the peace treaty between Egypt and Israel (1979), the novel depicts a romance between Sami, the first Egyptian-Christian student at the Hebrew University of Jerusalem, and Lital, an American-Jewish classmate from Seattle. The plot is complicated and fraught with factitious episodes at the end of which Sami finds himself arrested and tried for the murder of a Tel Aviv call girl. The Israeli chief-of-staff is forced to resign his post following revelations that he was involved in a sex scandal with this call girl, and the Israeli prime minister resigns as well. Miraculously acquitted after a long trial, Sami learns that Lital has left Israel in the meantime and returned to Seattle. In her farewell letter to him, she pledges her love for him and urges him to join her in Seattle. Hence the title, *Come with Me from Jerusalem*. The novel's message seems to be that an Arab-Jewish romance cannot flourish in the contested land in the toxic atmosphere of ethno-religious prejudice and hostility, even when the lovers are both outsiders who come from other countries—Egypt and the United States. However, as Al Aswany's novel *Chicago* demonstrates, neither can an Arab-Jewish romance flourish outside the boundaries of the conflicted land in a totally different setting such as American society. The intriguing question that arises is why did Abdel-Malek choose to write his novel in English rather than Arabic—his mother tongue. It is fair to assume that the medium of English afforded this author, who lives and works in Dubai, United Arab Emirates, the freedom to explore this taboo subject without exposing himself to backlash from conservative Arab audiences.

Arab-Israeli authors, and to some extent Palestinian authors living in the occupied territories,[24] have dealt more realistically with this sensitive topic in their works of fiction than their counterparts elsewhere in the Arab world. This is not surprising, considering that the Jewish population was expelled, or forced to migrate, from all Arab countries following the establishment of the Jewish state in 1948, with the result that only in Israel Arabs and Jews continue to live in close proximity to each other and to have social interaction. Prime examples are novels such as Atallah Mansour's *In a New Light* (1966); Usama Abu Ghush's *As a Jew Among Jews: A Love Story* (1995); Sayed Kashua's *Dancing Arabs* (2002); Nassib D. Bulos's *Jerusalem Crossroads* (2003), and Ayman Sikseck's *To Jaffa* (2010).[25] All these novels tell of a love story between an Arab man and a Jewish woman: the forbidden romance flourishes for a while but ultimately collapses under the pressure of numerous trials and tribulations experienced from both sides of the divide.

Jerusalem Crossroads, written in English by the Palestinian-Lebanese journalist Nassib D. Bulos,[26] is set in Mandatory Palestine during the turbulent years of 1946 and 1947. The protagonist, Nabeel Haddad, a prominent Palestinian journalist with close ties to both the British authorities and the Palestinian leadership, has a Jewish lover named Leah Ravinsky, who is a Zionist activist with ties to the Jewish underground (the Irgun paramilitary organization). Recruited to spy on Nabeel and gather information about the activities of the Palestinian leadership, Leah falls in love with him and he with her. Nabeel sees in Leah the woman of his dreams, and she sees in him a sensitive and sophisticated man who is "not a hypocrite, and what is more important, he seems to regard the Jews as human beings, and not as members of an inferior race" (p. 90). However, she is torn between conflicting loyalties: to succeed in her mission, she has to betray Nabeel's trust in her, and if she fails in her mission, she will be regarded as a traitor to the Jewish cause. She can't move in with Nabeel, even though they are both ready to make a commitment to each other, because that would be seen as proof of complicity on her part and her life would be at risk. "I love you, but it is hell," she says to Nabeel, to which he replies, "It may be that someday we will be able to proclaim our love to the world. Palestinian or Jewish ... we both belong to the Semitic world" (p. 125). Although Nabeel suspects that Leah is connected to the Jewish underground, he resolves to compartmentalize his love for her so that it will not interfere with his professional or political life. For a while, the star-crossed lovers manage to hide the true nature of their relationship from their families, friends, and colleagues. Leah is aware that even if she acts with the utmost discretion, sooner or later she would become known as "Nabeel's whore" and a scandal would break out: "To the outsider, love would not change the picture, nor would it sanctify their relationship" (p. 91). When Nabeel asks a British officer to guard his house during Leah's visit with him, the officer, who knows about their affair, cynically remarks, "This Palestinian-Jewish romance is turning into another Romeo and Juliet" (p. 174). And when asked to help fly them to Cyprus so that they can get married there, the British officer warns him, "My friend, you should have your head examined. You are courting disaster" (p. 182). Undaunted, Nabeel tells Leah that he is prepared to marry her, and if necessary, leave the country and settle elsewhere. But Leah rejects his offer. "Our destiny is here in this country" (p. 146), she argues. Although she appreciates the sacrifice he is willing to make for her, she fears that nothing but misery can come from their love: "We are no longer able to live as human beings. We are no more than cogs in an infernal machine, victims of circumstance" (p. 187).

The wave of terror and chaos that sweeps across Mandatory Palestine as the British prepare to evacuate their forces from the country makes Nabeel realize the impossibility of his marriage to Leah, unless he departs from Palestine permanently rather than temporarily. He is aware that Leah shares his view that life for them as a couple is not feasible, despite their intense love for each other. The novel ends on a gloomy note: "They had come to be resigned to the reality of the rift between Jew and Palestinian. There had been too much blood, too much hate, and they both knew that this was only the tip of the iceberg, and that the explosion, the final explosion would come later. They also both realized that even if married and living in some other country, Palestine would continue to haunt them, and that their love would turn sour, and that it was best if they were to part with love instead of hate in their hearts" (p. 189). Leah returns to Rehavia, the Jewish section of Jerusalem, consoling herself with the joyous memories of the time they spent together, while Nabeel remains in the Arab section of the city, reassuring himself that the pain of separation would ease with time and that meanwhile he should return to his work, for the Palestinian tragedy is far from over.

Unlike Bulos's *Jerusalem Crossroads*, which depicts forbidden love between an Arab man and a Jewish woman in Mandatory Palestine before the Nakba ("the Catastrophe," the Arabic term for the loss of Palestine in the 1948 war), when the Arab population was a majority and the Jewish community a minority, the novel *As a Jew Among Jews: A Love Story*, written in Hebrew by the Arab-Israeli author Usama Abu Ghush,[27] explores forbidden love between an Arab man and a Jewish woman in the State of Israel, where the Arabs have become a minority living among the Jewish majority. In both of these novels the mixed couples find their soulmates in each other, but their loving relationship falls apart under the pressure of ethno-religious tensions and hostilities. However, in *Jerusalem Crossroads* the Arab lover does not try to integrate into Jewish society and does not suffer from an identity crisis, personal or national, whereas in Abu Ghush's novel the Arab lover struggles with a dual identity: at work, he is known to his boss and coworkers as an Arab, and as such he is often subjected to disparaging remarks and humiliating experiences; after work, when he is with Racheli, his Jewish lover, he pretends that he is a Jew called Sami to her friends and neighbors. This protagonist, whose Arabic name remains anonymous—an important detail suggesting that he can be any Arab living in Israel—moves between two societies: Israeli society, where he is marginalized, and Arab society, where his roots, family, and culture are located. He is aware that he lives with a dual identity and it bothers him, robbing him of peace of mind and a stable sense of self. His masquerade under a Jewish identity is partly motivated by his desire to be accepted into Israeli society, and partly by Racheli's insistence that he should not reveal who he really is to her family and friends so as to spare her trouble and criticism. In this respect she is diametrically opposed to Leah, the Jewish lover in *Jerusalem Crossroads*, who does not impose any conditions on her Arab lover and is willing to sacrifice her own happiness for his sake. To safeguard their secret, Racheli and Sami live in a bubble, insulating themselves from the outside world in the cocoon of their apartment.

After living with Racheli under an assumed identity for twelve years—a period that begins a few years after the Six-Day War (1967), extends through the October 1973 War, and concludes with the invasion of Lebanon in 1982—Sami's attempts to live "as a Jew among Jews" fail, and he realizes that he has no future with Racheli: "Marriage was out of the question. Neither of us considered converting to the other's religion, nor did we demand it of each other. Racheli argued, and I agreed with her, that even if we had a civil marriage, people in Israel would harass us and make our lives miserable. In order to escape such an ordeal, we would have to live abroad, and to do so we would have to be millionaires."[28] By now thirty-seven years old, Sami longs to raise a family and be a father. Having a child with Racheli is not an option: "It was clear to me that even without marriage, according to the law in Israel, if the mother is Jewish then the child is considered Jewish. This frightened me because it means that the child would belong to the state—they could take him away from me. I knew of many cases of Jewish women who converted to Islam, bore children, and later on—usually under pressure from the wife's family or fanatic Jewish agencies—left the husband and took the children with them. Moreover, in due course the child would be drafted into the army and become a soldier—I was afraid of that too."[29] Torn between his mind and his heart, the need to separate from Racheli and the desire to stay with her, he finally decides to leave her. He travels to Germany, where his sister introduces him to one of her Arab girlfriends, and they become engaged to be married. However, he is tormented by feelings of guilt about Racheli, uncertain whether he left her because she was ten years his senior and he wanted a younger woman, or because the constant social and political pressures that they faced have undermined their relationship. All he is certain of is that he hated the assumed name he had to adopt all those years, and missed his real name, and wanted to be called by the name his father had given him on the day he was born.

It would seem that all the characters in the works of Arab-Israeli authors who enter into this taboo relationship suffer the same fate: breakup and heartache. In the novel *Dancing Arabs*,[30] a semi-autobiographical account by Sayed Kashua, a fiction writer and journalist whose medium of expression is Hebrew, the Arab protagonist is again nameless, a fact suggesting that he can be any Arab living in Israel. He receives a scholarship to study at an elite Jewish boarding school in Jerusalem, where he falls in love with a Jewish classmate, Naomi, an orphan whose father, an IDF officer, died in a car accident. They hang out together throughout the eleventh and twelfth grades, and though Naomi admits that she loves him, she warns him not to get too attached to her because their relationship will end when they graduate from high school, "otherwise, Mother will throw me out of the house" (p. 124). When she can no longer hide this relationship from her mother and tells her that she has an Arab boyfriend, her mother responds that she would rather have a lesbian for a daughter than someone who dates Arabs.

As a member of a left-wing political party called Ratz,[31] Naomi believes in humanistic values: "She talked a lot about human beings as human beings. About how there was no difference between national groups, how individuals should be judged on their own merits, and how you shouldn't look at a whole group as if everyone were the same. She said that in every nation there are good people and bad people" (pp. 116–117). Open-minded and sympathetic, she defies prejudice and bigotry. However, the couple's relationship is not free of tensions. For example, on Memorial Day for the Fallen Soldiers, Naomi is furious that her Arab boyfriend did not stand at attention during the memorial siren. When she asks him for the reason, he replies simply, "I'm not Jewish" (p. 114).

Kashua's nameless protagonist, like Sami in Abu Ghush's *As a Jew Among Jews: A Love Story*, is desperate to integrate into Israeli society. Soon after arriving from his village at the boarding school he undergoes a total transformation: he shaves his mustache, wears clothes purchased at Jewish stores, buys records and books in Hebrew, changes his eating habits, and learns how to pronounce the consonant *P* properly. His efforts are successful: "I look more Israeli than the average Israeli. I'm always pleased when Jews tell me this. 'You don't look like an Arab at all' they say. Some people claim it's a racist thing to say, but I've always taken it as a compliment, a sign of success. That's what I've always wanted to be, after all: a Jew. I've worked hard at it, and I've finally pulled it off" (p. 91). Although he constantly moves between two societies, two cultures, and two languages, his efforts to separate his personal identity from his national identity ultimately fail.

The protagonist is so preoccupied with the relationship with Naomi that he neglects his studies and fails to prepare for the matriculation examinations. Naomi, on the other hand, is focused on her future: "She said she was planning to study psychology. She was going to ask for a deferral of her army service so she could study first, and she had to get good grades on her finals. When the exams were over, we'd split up; I knew that. That's what her mother wanted. She said boarding school was a world apart, and as long as we were there she didn't mind that her daughter had an Arab boyfriend. She said she had nothing against me, except it was too bad my name wasn't Reuben or David" (p. 122).

Deeply depressed over the impending end of their relationship, the protagonist swallows a bottle of tranquilizers and is taken to the hospital to have his stomach pumped. When his father arrives there, he yells at him, blaming his self-destructive behavior on his Jewish girlfriend: "It's all because of that bitch of his, the Jewish whore" (p. 119). The son is aware that his father is actually concerned about his own reputation, fearing that he would be criticized and blamed for his son's suicide attempt. Resentful of his authoritarian and brutal father, the protagonist confesses: "How I hated him then. And I hated the guidance counselor even more. She wanted me to stop loving Naomi, or at least try to love Salwa, an Arab girl at school. She was pretty and smart, that's what the counselor kept telling me" (p. 125).

After flunking his final exams at the boarding school, the protagonist escapes to Jerusalem, where he becomes a squatter in a friend's dorm room at the Hebrew University and supports himself by working as an attendant in an institution for the retarded. He is still stuck on Naomi, whom he hasn't seen again after the last day of school. Gloomily, he recounts: "Sometimes, when I didn't want to go back to the dorms, I'd go to the university, look for the psych department, and wait outside for Naomi. I had tried to talk to her at first, to tell her I had a job, and money, and might invite her to a restaurant sometime. But she was always busy. Sometimes I followed her from a distance and tried to find out whether she had a new boyfriend yet. I wanted to know if she was as unhappy as I was. Maybe she still loved me and missed me; maybe it was only because of her mother that we'd split up. But she almost always looked happy, and she was surrounded by friends as she went to the cafeteria or the library" (p. 138). Conflicted and aimless, he eventually drifts into marriage to an Arab woman from his village, but her dark skin makes him cringe, and he soon dreams about taking a lover.

Naomi has moved on, blending with ease into her new social environment, her sense of identity clear, secure, and stable. Her Arab lover, however, is left dangling behind, unable to integrate into Israeli society on the one hand, and unable to feel at home in his own Arab village on the other hand. Having lost his authentic self, he has not figured out yet who he is and where he belongs.

Like Sayed Kashua, his younger contemporary Ayman Sikseck, in his novel *To Jaffa*,[32] also written in Hebrew, depicts the complex and fragmented social, political, and psychological realities of the third generation of Palestinians since the establishment of the State of Israel in 1948. In this novel the narrator-protagonist, again nameless, is an Arab from the mixed Arab-Jewish city of Jaffa who studies literature at the Hebrew University in Jerusalem and writes his life story in his journal in Hebrew. He has internalized the codes of behavior, dress, and language of the dominant Jewish culture in order to be accepted into Israeli society and has acquired a hybrid identity that allows him to move smoothly between Arab and Israeli societies without attracting attention by members of either group. He is involved in two relationships: one with Sharihan, a Muslim woman who becomes engaged to another man, and the other with Nitzan, a Jewish woman who serves in the IDF and later goes into security services. When the protagonist travels with Nitzan on a bus to the movies in Tel Aviv, their relationship is put to the test. An old Arab woman with a large shopping bag gets on the bus and some of the passengers, including Nitzan, become suspicious that she is a suicide bomber. "'Are you thinking what I'm thinking?' Nitzan took my hand and entwined her fingers in mine. 'What are you thinking?' I feigned ignorance. 'It looks suspicious to me.' 'What do you mean suspicious?' I felt my cheeks reddening. 'Because she is an Arab, she looks suspicious?' Nitzan looked at me shocked and remained silent for a while. 'What?!' she finally said. 'Did you see the bag she's holding? That's why she looks suspicious. Anyway, look around, everyone is frightened.'"[33] Eventually forced to empty her bag, whose contents prove harmless, the Arab woman gets off the bus, cursing in Arabic. The disturbing incident prevents the protagonist from enjoying the movie, and he leaves Nitzan at the cinema and returns to Jaffa, where he tells his father, "Nitzan won't be coming around anymore."[34] The incident on the bus brings the couple's fundamental differences to the fore and terminates their relationship. The protagonist's inability to share his girlfriend's fear and anxiety and the shame he feels for not defending the Arab woman are contrasted with Nitzan's profound suspicion and apprehension and her inability to relate to his experience. These irreconcilable differences create an emotional distance between them that ultimately separates them.

The only work of fiction in which an Arab-Jewish love story ends on a hopeful note is Atallah Mansour's *In a New Light*, the first novel to be written in Hebrew by an Arab-Israeli.[35] The narrative, which highlights the issue of a false/dual identity and its hidden pitfalls, centers around an orphan Arab boy named Yusuf who is taken, out of compassion, into the home of Baruch Mizrachi, the Jewish partner of his slain father. A few years later, Mizrachi's children run away from home to join a youth group in a kibbutz and take Yusuf with them. Calling himself Yossi Mizrachi and passing himself off as a Jew, he grows up in this kibbutz and tries to fit into their pioneering, socialist society, but fails. He leaves it in his mid-twenties and joins another, more revolutionary kibbutz. There he meets Rivkah, a kindergarten teacher who immigrated to Israel from California. Although Rivkah is married, she embarks on a love affair with Yossi, whom she takes for a Yemenite Jew.

2 DANGEROUS LIAISONS: ARAB-JEWISH ROMANTIC RELATIONSHIPS   31

What draws these opposite characters together? As it turns out, they have a lot in common: Rivkah, with her blue eyes and blond hair, does not look Jewish and can easily pass for a gentile. In fact, she took advantage of her outward appearance and made such pretenses more than once during her youth in California, when she was anxious to blend in mainstream American society. Her story mirrors that of Yossi, who hides his Arab identity and masquerades as an Oriental Jew in order to blend in Israeli society. Yossi, a lonely person who grew up with no ties to his family of origin, yearns for intimacy and tenderness, and Rivkah, who is a nurturing figure (as reflected in her occupation as a kindergarten teacher), yearns to have a child that she can mother, a child that her husband, Yehuda, refuses to give her. No wonder, then, that Rivkah and Yossi immediately feel a strong affinity with each other.

Their romance blossoms under the nose of Rivkah's husband. But Rivkah soon tires of leading a double life; she confesses to her husband about the affair and breaks up with Yossi. When Yossi inquires why she revealed their affair, she replies, "I simply had to. I couldn't go on living a false life, a double life" (p. 108). Yossi fails to see how this plain truth applies to his own situation as well. He feels hopelessly lonely and rejected. "Being lonely," he admits, "was the normal condition of my life. ... My life was a salt sea, a desolate wilderness" (p. 99). To a great extent, his loneliness is the result of his adopting a false identity: to safeguard his secret, he must keep to himself and avoid forming any close relationships. But his false identity is ultimately exposed when he asks the kibbutz to accept him as a full-fledged member. The kibbutz, knowing very little about him, conducts a background investigation and discovers that he is actually an Arab named Yusuf. He is then told that his candidacy for a full-fledged membership is put on hold to give the kibbutz time to think things over and see him "in a new light" (hence the novel's title). Suddenly he, too, begins to see things in a new light: that the kibbutz's slogans of a world revolution, an egalitarian society, brotherhood of man, and peaceful coexistence are merely lofty words and fairy tales about the love of humanity irrespective of nationality and geography. Even his relationship with Rivkah appears to him in a new light now, and he resents her for misleading him that she loves him and then deserting him. As for Rivkah, she is shocked to learn that he has lied to her about his true identity and violated her trust in him. "You have been standing on the stage playing a magnificent part and making fools of us all" (p. 135), she angrily confronts him. In his defense, Yossi argues, "I was put on the stage from the day I was born and must go

32   D. COHEN-MOR

on acting if I don't want to fall off" (p. 135). But Rivkah denounces him: "You are a traitor to your people. You have abandoned them and joined a Jewish kibbutz" (p. 136).

Wanting to know where he stands, Yossi is not willing to wait indefinitely to hear whether the kibbutz decides to accept him as a full-fledged member, and presses for an answer. His case is brought up for discussion in the kibbutz general assembly, where the members face a historic decision: to admit an Arab as a full-fledged member of their society, which is egalitarian but Jewish, or not? After heated arguments for and against, they strike a compromise: "Nothing which has been said here will be put on record. The kibbutz will simply admit one more member, neither Jew nor Arab, and that's that" (p. 175). This hollow victory leaves a bitter taste in Yossi's mouth. He takes comfort in the arms of Rivkah who, in the meantime, has reconciled with him and left her husband for him. Her consoling words to him are: "I want your child. ... He will make the Revolution" (p. 176).

Atallah Mansour's *In a New Light* is the only novel that does not end on a heartbreaking note for the Arab-Jewish couple and in which this couple's romance is not condemned by their social environment, presumably because they live in a kibbutz and not in a city or a village. As noted earlier, Bulos's *Jerusalem Crossroad* was written in English and all the other novels by Arab-Israeli authors discussed above were written in Hebrew. This begs the question of whether using a different medium of expression than Arabic afforded these authors the freedom to deal with this taboo subject. Would they have dared to depict a love story between an Arab and a Jew in Arabic (i.e., for Arab readers)? Judging by the paucity of works on this topic in modern Arabic fiction, it seems reasonable to conclude that they would not.

As for Arab women writers, much like their male counterparts, they have been largely silent on this subject. The struggle for acceptance as authors in their own right generally discourages them from addressing sensitive issues. Nevertheless, occasionally one encounters a female-authored work of fiction featuring an Arab-Jewish romance. An intriguing example is the short story "Forbidden Talk," written in Arabic by the Palestinian woman writer Mysoon Assadi.[36] In this story, the protagonist, Jihan, confides in her two close female friends about her secret love affairs. Although she is a married woman with children, she has intimate relationships with other men; one of them is Ezra, her Jewish boss at work. As her shocked friends listen, she describes her passionate affair with him in vivid detail:

2 DANGEROUS LIAISONS: ARAB-JEWISH ROMANTIC RELATIONSHIPS

At work every day, I see and feel Ezra, the general executive of the company, while he looks at my body lustfully. ... I know and can see that the lust in his eyes will eventually kill him. He's tried repeatedly to voice his feelings, but he doesn't dare. His position of authority betrays him each time he tries. I look back at him coolly, anticipating what may happen. I admire his strong character very much. He runs a company with six hundred clerks and employees. I also adore his Eastern appearance. I think he is of Moroccan origin. He has been watching me for months and I enjoy it. I know exactly why he fears me and why, when I'm around, his boldness is replaced by hesitation. He is afraid of getting close to an Arab girl. He fears my response. To tell you the truth, I was getting fed up with his faltering. I took the initiative to break down the barrier between us. I paved the ground before him so he could approach me safely. And, after a few days, Ezra got in my bed. The storm of his love for me swept him to me. He was propelled toward me by a repressed, invincible power. He bent over and kissed the bottom of my feet and he loved the moments of my ecstasy when I was satisfied and turned from a wild lioness into a peaceful, spoiled cat. (pp. 58–59)

As soon as Jihan finishes describing her affair with Ezra, she moves on to her romance with Emil, and before him with Richard. Unabashedly, she tells her dumbfounded friends that every day, after her husband drinks up his bottle of alcohol in front of the TV and then passes out, she goes to her room, locks the door, takes off her clothes, and picks from a list of lovers who will share the night with her. Then she retrieves her "friend" from his hiding place under her bed pillow and has a wonderful time with him—until the battery runs out. Only then does the reader realize that Jihan's secret love affairs are merely figments of her imagination and that her "friend" is a vibrator. As she parts from her female friends, she announces, "Today I have my home to myself. My children are at school, my husband is at work, and I have a date with Abdul Haleem Hafez" (p. 61).[37] While the story turns out to be about sexual fantasies, the fact that an Arab heroine daydreams about a Jewish lover—however stereotyped and disparaging his depiction here might be—shows that the prevailing taboo on romance across ethnoreligious lines invites people to defy it, if not in reality then by the sheer power of imagination.

Another female-authored work of fiction depicting an Arab-Jewish romance is the novel *Habibi* (Arabic for "my darling," 1997),[38] written in English for young adults by the Arab-American poet and writer Naomi Shihab Nye. *Habibi* tells the story of Liyana Abboud, an adolescent girl from St. Louis who moves with her Palestinian father and

American mother to Jerusalem, where she meets Omer, an Israeli-Jewish boy, and the two of them fall in love with each other. Set in the period following the Oslo Accords between Israel and the Palestinians (1993), this semi-autobiographical novel offers a sensitive and balanced portrayal of the prejudices, grievances, suspicions, and fears that members of both communities need to overcome in order to develop ties of friendship. While Omer's mother forbids him to associate with Liyana or visit an Arab village, Liyana's parents, being themselves a mixed couple, are more open-minded; he gains their approval and is heartily embraced by Liyana's paternal grandmother, Sitti, who sees in him the power of healing. In the final, climactic scene, the grandmother reads Omer's fortune in his cup of tea as he sits together with Liyana's family in a restaurant by the Sea of Galilee. She says: "You will need to be brave. There are hard days coming. There are hard words waiting in people's mouths to be spoken. There are walls. You can't break them. Just find doors in them. See?... You already have. Here we are, together" (p. 270). The narrative ends on a hopeful note for change in Palestinian–Israeli relations and for peaceful coexistence. As a children's book, the educational value of this novel is inestimable, as it targets young readers whose minds are impressionable and can be easily influenced.

Works written by Israeli-Jewish authors about romantic relationships between Arabs and Jews by far outnumber those written by Arab authors. In a country where the Arab-Israeli conflict has dominated everyday life and constituted an underlying condition of existence, Arab-Jewish relations are a perennial topic of writing. The theme of forbidden romance serves as a lens through which the writer examines core issues in the relations between the two antagonistic sides, central among them are the Israeli's view of the Arab other, the Israeli's self-definition in relation to the Arab other, and the Israeli's connection to the land and its past. Some pertinent examples are Amos Oz's novella *Nomad and Viper* (1963), A. B. Yehoshua's novel *The Lover* (1977), Shimon Ballas's novel *A Locked Room* (1980), Savyon Liebrecht's short story "A Room on the Roof" (1986), Sami Michael's novel *A Trumpet in the Wadi* (1987), Michal Peleg's short story "The Good Jewess" (1996), Eli Amir's novel *Yasmine* (2005), and Dorit Rabinyan's novel *All the Rivers* (2014).[39] In all these works of fiction, the forbidden relationship eventually falls apart, ending in heartache, breakup, or death. In Amos Oz's *Nomad and Viper*, a young kibbutz woman, Geula, who has an ambiguous sexual encounter with a Bedouin, is bitten by a snake and dies.[40] In Shimon Ballas's *A Locked Room*, Sa'id, an Arab member of the Israeli Communist Party, and Smadar, a Jewish female member, have a long, complicated, and painful love affair; despite their deep feelings for each other and the slogans of Arab-Jewish friendship inculcated in them by the party, they break up and go their separate ways. In Sami Michael's *A Trumpet in the Wadi*, Alex, a young Russian-Jewish immigrant, is killed in the 1982-armed conflict in Lebanon just days before his marriage to Huda, an Arab-Israeli woman who is pregnant with his child. In Dorit Rabinyan's *All the Rivers*, a love affair blossoms between Liat, an Israeli-Jewish woman, and Hilmi, a Palestinian-Muslim man, when they meet in New York City, but Liat ends their love affair upon her return to Israel and soon after Hilmi drowns in the sea of Jaffa. In Eli Amir's *Yasmine*, the love between Nuri, an Iraqi-born Israeli Jew, and Yasmin, a Palestinian-Christian woman from East Jerusalem, remains unrequited, as they are unable to reconcile their conflicting loyalties and national aspirations, and she flees from him to Paris. Similarly, in Savyon Liebrecht's "A Room on the Roof,"[41] as well as in Michal Peleg's "The Good Jewess,"[42] the erotic/sexual encounter between a Jewish woman (a housewife and a lawyer respectively) and an Arab man (a construction worker and a villager respectively) ends abruptly when the Arab, who suffers indignities at work (in Liebrecht's story) and the demolition of his house by the Israeli authorities (in Peleg's story), walks away from the Jewish woman. Judging by all these somber endings, it would seem that Israeli society is not ready yet for intimate relationships between Arabs and Jews, and that these relationships are untenable and ultimately collapse under the pressure of the social and political realities.

A. B. Yehoshua's novel *The Lover*,[43] set in Israel immediately after the October 1973 War, was the first work of fiction to break the taboo on sex in the depiction of an Arab-Jewish relationship in Hebrew literature. Naim, a teenage Arab boy who works for Adam, a well-to-do Jewish garage owner living in Haifa, and Dafi, Adam's rebellious teenage daughter, are both lonely and adrift, and when they find themselves alone in Adam's apartment, their curiosity and passion get the better of them and they make love for the first time in their lives. When Adam discovers what happened, he decides to remove Naim immediately from proximity to Dafi by taking him back to his remote Arab village in the Upper Galilee. The two youngsters, still reeling from their first sexual experience, are thus separated, with little chance of seeing each other again. The novel, whose main focus is Adam's search for his wife's lost Jewish lover, reveals the deep-rooted tensions within family, between generations, and between Jews and Arabs.

No Hebrew work of fiction has shattered the taboo on sex between Arabs and Jews as dramatically as Dorit Rabinyan's *All the Rivers*.[44] The novel depicts the torrid love affair of an Israeli-Jewish translator, Liat, with a Palestinian artist, Hilmi, during a frigid winter in New York City shortly after the terrorist attacks of 11 September 2001. The narrative abounds in graphic sexual scenes which, though lyrically depicted, are unprecedented in Hebrew fiction on this topic. While the lovers enjoy exploring the city together, reminiscing about their childhoods, and visiting American friends, they constantly clash when it comes to discussing politics, as they do not see eye to eye on the solution for the Israeli–Palestinian conflict: Hilmi supports the binational-state solution, while Liat supports the two-state solution. This is not the only source of tension in their relationship. Liat hides Hilmi's existence from her family in Israel and from her Jewish friends in New York. Whenever she calls her parents, she asks Hilmi to "disappear from her life for ten minutes," lest they should hear his voice with his thick Arabic accent in the background and discover the scandalous affair. Offended, Hilmi demands to know: "What am I to you?... I'm your secret Arab lover?" (p. 126). When she tacitly acknowledges this fact, he adds cynically, "Arab, and secret ... and temporary" (p. 127). But Hilmi gives her a taste of her own medicine when his brother comes to visit him and, along with several Arab friends, they all have dinner together. A heated argument about Israel ensues between Hilmi's brother and Liat, but Hilmi abandons her and does not come to her defense. Leaving the table in tears, she realizes that at the critical moment Hilmi chooses for his primary identity—his brother and his compatriots—just as she does.

All the Rivers is not a story of love conquering all. As the date of her departure from New York back to Israel draws near, Liat must decide whether she is willing to risk estrangement from her family and community for the love of this man. As it turns out, she is not. She says goodbye to her Palestinian lover and resumes her life in Israel among her fellow Jews. Shortly afterward, Hilmi, feeling homesick, arrives in Ramallah for a visit with his family. His unfulfilled wishes, as he has once told Liat, are to learn how to drive, how to shoot, and how to swim. On a day trip to the beach of Jaffa, he drowns at sea while attempting to save his nephew's life.

All the Rivers has been touted as "a Romeo and Juliet story for our times" in that it is about forbidden love that ends in tragedy. However, Shakespeare's characters are prepared to sacrifice everything for each other, whereas Rabinyan's characters are not: Liat flees from her Arab lover to Israel, and Hilmi dies not for the sake of his Jewish lover but for the sake of his nephew. It is pertinent to note that the book was recommended to be added to the required literature curriculum of Israeli high schools by a panel of educators and academics, but Israel's Education Ministry rejected this suggestion on the grounds that it could encourage intermarriage and that it depicts IDF soldiers as sadistic war criminals. Rabinyan herself believes that the decision to disqualify her novel from high school literature classes stems from the fact that she portrays the Arab other with humanity: "He is a Palestinian and a full human. That is the power of the book and the reason for it to be banned."[45] However, other Israeli authors before her, both male and female, have portrayed the Palestinian with humanity and their works have not been excluded from high school literature classes. Eventually, after the ban sparked a storm over censorship, the Education Ministry announced that the book may be studied in advanced literature classes in the context of alternative appraisals, but not as part of the regular school curriculum.

Curiously, the copyright page of the book carries a disclaimer saying, "*All the Rivers* is a work of fiction. Names, characters, places, and incidents are the product of the author's imagination and are used fictitiously. Any resemblance to actual events, locales, or persons, living or dead, is entirely coincidental." At the same time, the book is dedicated to Hassan Hourani (1974–2003), a Palestinian artist whose life was cut short when he drowned while swimming in the sea of Jaffa. A eulogy/farewell letter to him, which Rabinyan wrote and published in *The Guardian* in 2004,[46] reveals that she was romantically involved with him when the two of them lived in New York City. The long letter provides intimate details about their relationship and Hourani's life and work. The similarities between the characters, places, and incidents described in her farewell letter and those depicted in her book are so striking that it is impossible to avoid the conclusion that *All the Rivers*, labeled as a novel, is in fact a memoir. Why the disclaimer then? Was the author embarrassed to be identified as Liat, an Israeli-Jewish woman who has a torrid love affair with a Palestinian-Muslim man? The disclaimer appears all the more implausible in light of the fact that her farewell letter preceded the publication of her book by ten years during which the author reportedly suffered from writer's block. It would seem that the fears of the protagonist, Liat, which drive her to hide the existence of her Arab lover from her family, friends, and community, essentially reflect the fears of the author herself.

Unlike the literary works discussed above, where the lovers are a Jewish woman and an Arab man, in Sami Michael's *A Trumpet in the Wadi* the lovers are a Jewish man and an Arab woman.[47] Set in Haifa in the months preceding the 1982-armed conflict in Lebanon, the novel tells the story of Huda and her younger sister Mary, two fatherless Christian Arabs, polar opposites in appearance and personality, who live in the wadi—the Arab quarter in the Jewish city of Haifa. After Huda rejects a marriage proposal from a self-seeking Arab suitor, she sinks into a deep depression and resigns herself to a spinster's life, until Alex, a young Russian-Jewish immigrant, moves into the room on the roof of her building. Alex plays the trumpet, and his stirring melodies find their way into Huda's soul and reawaken her passion and joy of living. As a new immigrant, Alex does not speak Hebrew well and Huda, who is fluent in Hebrew, volunteers to teach him the language. This scenario is contrary to what is commonly depicted in works of fiction on the topic, where the linguistic imbalance is usually in favor of the Jewish character, who has mastery of the Hebrew language, whereas the Arab character speaks broken Hebrew or none at all.

Before long, the two become lovers and Alex proposes to her. He does not mind that Huda is an Arab, saying, "What sort of Jew I am? I do not even know holidays. I mix up Purim and Kippurim. I could not understand one word when Mother and Papa talked Yiddish in Russia. I also did not want to come to Israel, not at all. Mother fixed up everything" (p. 145). His attitude is consistent with the findings of a survey conducted in Israel in 2014, which reported that opposition to intermarriage was lowest among immigrants from the former Soviet Union, presumably because they did not undergo the religious and Zionist education that more established Israeli-Jews received.[48] As for Huda, like many Arab-Israelis, she belongs to two worlds: the world of her Arab family, culture, and society, and the world of Jewish culture and society. Her favorite writer is the Hebrew poet Yehuda Amichai, and she works in a Jewish travel agency where she is well liked by her boss and coworkers. Most importantly, Huda has a supportive family: her mother, sister, and grandfather acknowledge that Alex is a good man and accept her decision to marry him, despite his Jewish identity. Their tolerance is largely attributable to the fact that they are Christian Arabs of Egyptian-Coptic background, rather than Muslim Arabs. While Huda's Jewish coworkers are sympathetic to her plan to marry Alex, her boss wonders aloud, "Why does she need such trouble in this fucked-up country?... I wouldn't have wished it on her" (p. 169). Huda is so devoted to Alex that she is even willing to convert to Judaism for his sake. But a few days before they are set to get married, the 1982-armed conflict in Lebanon breaks out, and Alex, who is called to the front, is killed in action. Huda's

2 DANGEROUS LIAISONS: ARAB-JEWISH ROMANTIC RELATIONSHIPS

dream of building a home with the father of the child she is carrying is shattered. Standing at his fresh grave in the cemetery, which is filled with many other bereaved and inconsolable people, she pours out her heart:

> So you see Alex, ... this will probably decide the issue. I mean the child's future. If I bring him up in the Arab society, will I have to tell him, before he hears it from others, that he was fathered out of wedlock by a Jew? Or should I raise him in Jewish society? In another eighteen years I will not be attractive and strong like Adina [a coworker], sustained with warm care by parents and lover. Your mother even snatched away your trumpet before she returned the room to Abu-Nakhla [the landlord]. You can imagine what my position will be when the time comes to send your son to another war. He will want to join an elite unit. All his life he will try to prove himself, because his mother is Arab, and he will be a stranger among both Arabs and Jews. (pp. 243–244)

The dilemma that Huda faces concerning her child's future shows how hard it is to raise a child of a mixed, Arab-Jewish parentage in Israel. The novel does not disclose what decision Huda makes, whether to give birth to the child or to abort it, thus avoiding a clear-cut resolution. This indeterminate or inconclusive ending suggests that the author sees no viable solution to the exceedingly complex and prolonged Arab-Israeli conflict.

A romantic entanglement between a Jewish man and an Arab woman is also the focus of Eli Amir's novel *Yasmine*,[49] which is set in Jerusalem in the aftermath of the Six-Day War (1967). Nuri Imari, an Iraqi-born Israeli Jew who is an Arabist by training, is appointed an advisor on Arab affairs for the Israeli government; his task is to help restore normalization to the recently reunited city by reaching out to the Arabs of East Jerusalem. Nuri describes himself as an "*ibn-Arab* Jew," referring to his dual cultural orientation as a Jew from an Arab land who loves the East but also admires the wonders of the West: "I listen to classical music in the morning and Arabic music in the evening," he says. "I'm a bird of passage wandering between two worlds, a foot here and a foot there, and sometimes my feet get mixed up" (p. 379). Yasmine, the Sorbonne-educated daughter of a wealthy Palestinian-Christian family from East Jerusalem, is a child psychologist who has just returned from several years of studying in Paris. When the two meet, Nuri finds himself falling in love with her, and she with him. But even this couple, who share a close cultural affinity with each other, cannot hold on to their relationship for long.

40 D. COHEN-MOR

After repeatedly suffering indignities at army checkpoints, Yasmine realizes that she is unable to adapt to the country that was once her home but now is under Israeli occupation, and that she is unwilling to live in it as a second-class citizen. As much as she loves Nuri and wants to be with him, she cannot give up her national identity–or escape from it. She therefore leaves Nuri and returns to Paris.

Interestingly, when Yasmine and Nuri first meet, she refuses to speak with him in Hebrew, even though she is fluent in it, having learned it in her childhood, and she also refuses to let Nuri speak with her in Arabic, in which he is fluent. Instead, she insists that they use English as a means of communication. This shows that although she has internalized an important cultural attribute of the Israeli other—the Hebrew language—she is as yet unwilling to accept the Israeli other. However, in her farewell letter to Nuri, she writes that she came to realize that he, too, has indissoluble ties to the land, a realization that implies an acceptance of the Israeli other: "During our few days of happiness I loved every moment of being with you, and for the first time sensed also your 'as-sumood,' your love for this soil, the sweat and blood with which you watered it. Your story and ours are more difficult than the judgment of Solomon. Here neither side will give in and no one will be spared" (pp. 443–444).

Described as "a novel of irreconcilable dualities,"[50] all the characters in this elaborate narrative of several subplots are either culturally divided or stand in opposition to each other. Whether they are Arab or Jewish, they must all come to terms with the reality that "this country has two histories, two languages, two cultures, two visions, two dreams. Anyone who tries to claim the whole thing will end up with nothing" (p. 421). It is worth noting that *Yasmine* was translated into Arabic by Hussein al-Sarag, deputy editor-in-chief of the Egyptian *October* magazine, and published in Egypt in 2007, where it was well received. While many Hebrew-language novels are translated around the world, rarely does an Israeli author get to see his work translated into Arabic and published in an Arab country. *Yasmine* was the fourth Hebrew-language novel ever published in Arabic translation in Egypt. In Israel, by contrast, many Arab authors are translated into Hebrew every year.

In conclusion, all the works of fiction, by Jewish as well as Arab authors, discussed above illustrate the great hardships—familial, cultural, religious, societal, national, and political—encountered in violating the taboo on love across ethno-religious lines. The romances depicted in these literary works are not stories of love conquering all: the characters are generally unable to make the leap and sacrifice everything for each other. Ultimately, the relationship collapses, ending in heartache, breakup, or death. Such complex issues and formidable dilemmas stamped the impossible love of Mahmoud Darwish and "Rita" and are reflected in the series of poems and prose passages that he dedicated to her.

NOTES

1. Etel Adnan, *Sitt Marie Rose* (Sausalito: Post-Apollo Press, 1982).
2. Jaap Timmer, "Dangerous Liaisons: Perceptions on Arab/Jewish Intermarriage in Israel." *Culture Matters* (9 August 2011), p. 1. https://culturematters.com. Accessed 20 November 2016.
3. "Most Israeli Jews, and Arabs, Oppose Intermarriage." *The Times of Israel* (22 August 2014), p. 1. http://www.timesofIsrael.com. Accessed 4 September 2016.
4. Ibid.
5. David K. Shipler, *Arab and Jew: Wounded Spirits in a Promised Land,* rev. ed. (New York: Broadway Books, 2015), p. 579.
6. Cited in Jonathan Cook, "In Israel, Intermarriage Viewed as Treason." *The Electronic Intifada* (25 September 2009), p. 2. https://electronicintifada. net. Accessed 28 August 2016.
7. Cited in Elizabeth Blade, "Married to Mohammed—Part IV." *Israel Today* (7 September 2012), pp. 1–2. http://www.israeltoday.co.il. Accessed 20 November 2016.
8. Cited in ibid., p. 2. Emphasis mine.
9. Ibid.
10. Cook, "In Israel, Intermarriage Viewed as Treason," pp. 2–4. See also Timmer, "Dangerous Liaisons," pp. 2–4.
11. Shipler, *Arab and Jew*, p. 580.
12. "Egyptian Mona Lisa" appears in *Yusuf Idris: The Piper Dies and Other Stories,* trans. Dalya Cohen-Mor with Francis Liardet (Potomac, MD: Sheba Press, 1992), pp. 1–25.
13. Yusuf Idris, *The Sinners*, trans. Kristin Peterson-Ishaq (Washington, DC: Three Continents Press, 1984).
14. Suleiman Fayyad, *Voices*, trans. Hosam Aboul-Ela (New York: Marion Boyars, 1993).
15. For further discussion of this topic, see Nidal M. al-Mousa, "The Arabic Bildungsroman: A Generic Appraisal," *International Journal of Middle East Studies* 25 (1993): 223–240.
16. For additional information on the Arabic female bildungsroman, see Dalya Abudi, *Mothers and Daughters in Arab Women's Literature: The Family Frontier* (Leiden: Brill, 2011), pp. 138–144.

17. Somaya Ramadan, *Leaves of Narcissus* (*Awraq al-narjis*, 2001), trans. Marilyn Booth (Cairo: American University in Cairo Press, 2002).
18. Ramziya Abbas al-Iryani, *Al-Ghariba* (The Stranger), in her collection *Al-Sama' tumtiru qutnan* (The Sky is Raining Cotton) (Sana'a, 1999).
19. Miral al-Tahawy, *Brooklyn Heights* (*Murtafa'at Bruklin*, 2010), trans. Sameh Salim (London: Faber and Faber, 2012).
20. *Far from Land* (*Ba'idan 'an al-ard*) appears in Ihsan Abd al-Quddus's collection *Shafatah* (Beirut, 1961). Trans. Trevor Le Gassick, in *Ihsan Abd al-Quddus: I Am Free and Other Stories* (Cairo: General Egyptian Book Organization, 1978), pp. 227–249. All citations are from this source.
21. Khalil Baydas, *Al-Warith* (1920; Ramallah: Alraqamia, 2011).
22. Alaa Al Aswany, *Chicago*, trans. Farouk Abdel Wahab (Cairo: American University in Cairo Press, 2007). All citations are from this source.
23. Kamal Abdel-Malek, *Come with Me from Jerusalem* (UAE, 2013).
24. In this work, I use the term Israeli-Arab or Arab-Israeli to refer to Arabs who live within Israeli borders and have Israeli citizenship, in contrast to those living in Gaza or the West Bank (or those who fled in 1948 or migrated elsewhere), to whom I refer as Palestinians.
25. In this sample, Usama Abu Ghush's novel and Ayman Sikseck's novel are not yet available in English translation.
26. Nassib D. Bulos, *Jerusalem Crossroads* (Beirut: Dar al-Nahar, 2003). All citations are from this source.
27. Usama Abu Ghush, *Ke-Yehudi bein yehudim: sipur ahava* (As a Jew Among Jews: A Love Story) (Raanana: Center for the Research of Arab Society in Israel, 1995). All citations are from this source.
28. Ibid., p. 146. Translation mine.
29. Ibid. Translation mine.
30. Sayed Kashua, *Dancing Arabs* (*Aravim rokdim*, 2002), trans. Miriam Shlesinger (New York: Grove Press, 2004). All citations are from this source.
31. Officially the movement for civil rights, it was active from 1973 until its formal merger into Meretz (another left-wing, social-democratic, and green political party) in 1997.
32. Ayman Sikseck, *El Yafo* (To Jaffa) (Tel Aviv: Yediot Ahronot and Hemed Books, 2010).
33. Ibid., p. 55. Translation mine.
34. Ibid., p. 58. Translation mine.
35. Atallah Mansour, *In a New Light* (*Be'or hadash*, 1966), trans. Abraham Birman (London: Vallentine Mitchell, 1969). All citations are from this source.
36. Maysoon Assadi, "Forbidden Talk," in *Loud Sounds from the Holy Land: Short Fiction by Palestinian Women*, ed. and trans. Jamal Assadi with Martha Moody (New York: Peter Lang, 2011), pp. 57–60. All citations are from this source.

37. The name of a famous Egyptian singer who died in the mid-1970s.
38. Naomi Shihab Nye, *Habibi* (New York: Simon Pulse, 1997). All citations are from this source.
39. This is not an exhaustive list but a sample of well-known works by leading Israeli-Jewish writers.
40. Amos Oz, *Nomad and Viper*, in his collection *Where the Jackals Howl and Other Stories*, trans. Nicholas de Lange and Philip Simpson (New York: Harcourt Brace Jovanovich, 1981), pp. 21–38.
41. Savyon Liebrecht, "A Room on the Roof," trans. Jeffrey M. Green, in her collection *Apples from the Desert* (New York: Feminist Press, 1998), pp. 39–63.
42. Michal Peleg, "The Good Jewess" ("Ha-Yehudiya ha-tova"), in her collection *Shir heres ve-sipurim aherim* (Ruin Song and Other Stories) (Tel Aviv: Ha-Kibbutz Ha-Meuhad, 1996), pp. 30–55.
43. A. B. Yehoshua, *The Lover* (*Ha-Me'ahev*, 1977), trans. Philip Simpson (New York: Doubleday, 1978).
44. Dorit Rabinyan, *All the Rivers* (*Gader haya*, 2014), trans. Jessica Cohen (New York: Random House, 2017). All citations are from this source.
45. Cited in Raf Sanchez, "Forbidden Israeli-Arab Love Story Sparks a Storm over Censorship." *The Telegraph* (11 January 2016). http://www.telegraph.co.uk. Accessed 11 September 2016. Rabinyan repeated this assertion at a presentation she gave at the Center for Israel Studies at American University, Washington, DC, on 20 April 2017.
46. Dorit Rabinyan, "The Exile's Return: Eulogy for Hassan Hourani." *The Guardian* (2 April 2004). http://www.theguardian.com/books. Accessed 16 September 2016.
47. Sami Michael, *A Trumpet in the Wadi* (*Hatsotsra ba-vadi*, 1987), trans. Yael Lotam (New York: Simon & Schuster, 1987). All citations are from this source.
48. "Most Israeli Jews, and Arabs, Oppose Intermarriage." *The Times of Israel* (22 August 2014). http://www.timesofIsrael.com. Accessed 4 September 2016.
49. Eli Amir, *Yasmine* (Hebrew, 2005), trans. Yael Lotan (London: Halban, 2012). All citations are from this source.
50. "Yasmin: A Novel of Irreconcilable Dualities." Posted 24 February 2012. http://jewishrefugees.blogspot.com. Accessed 28 November 2017.

CHAPTER 3

Self-Defining Memories: When Mahmoud Met "Rita"

Abstract This chapter describes the forbidden love between Darwish and Rita. Drawing on multiple sources, including the documentary film *Write Down, I Am an Arab*, newspaper articles, and published interviews, I provide an account of Rita's identity, background, and career, how she and Darwish met, what brought them together, and what drove them apart. I offer an explanation as to why, following their breakup, Rita became a leitmotif in Darwish's poetry. I highlight the power of first love as the main motive for this leitmotif, and also draw on the theory of "self-defining memories" in psychology to elucidate its function. This theory is especially pertinent here, given that Darwish's love for Rita was unrequited and ended in heartache.

Keywords Mahmoud Darwish and Rita—forbidden love story · Rita—identity, background, and career · Mahmoud Darwish's love poems—Rita leitmotif · Mahmoud Darwish—unrequited love

When the Arab-Israeli filmmaker, Ibtisam Mara'ana, set out to make a documentary film about Mahmoud Darwish, it was not so much out of a desire to celebrate his life and poetry as the voice of the Palestinian people as out of a personal need to find legitimation for her love affair with an Israeli-Jewish man in Darwish's own love affair with an Israeli-Jewish woman.[1]

© The Author(s) 2019
D. Cohen-Mor, *Mahmoud Darwish*,
https://doi.org/10.1007/978-3-030-24162-9_3

45

Her documentary film, *Write Down, I Am an Arab* (*Sajjil ana 'Arabi*), premiered at Tel Aviv's DocAviv film festival in May 2014, where it won the Audience Choice Award. The film presented the never-before-seen love letters that Darwish wrote to his Jewish lover, revealing a fascinating facet in the personality of the man whose poems came to represent Palestinian collective consciousness.

Mara'ana did not attempt to hide her ulterior motive for making the documentary film. In her director's statement, she candidly wrote: "Mahmoud Darwish is an icon of the Arab world. His words inspired millions around the world, shaped Palestinian identity, and helped galvanize generations of Palestinians to their cause. But what many people do not know is that his first love was a Jewish woman from Haifa. His poem 'Rita and the Rifle' has been very influential in my life. I too live in a relationship with a Jewish man and in the same reality of ongoing war and conflict that Darwish once lived. 'If Mahmoud Darwish, the Palestinian poet and refugee, fell in love with a Jewish girl and wrote her poetry, then so can I.' That was what I said to legitimize my love."[2]

A gifted movie and television screenwriter and director, Mara'ana was born in 1975 into a conservative Muslim family in the Arab village of Fureidis near Zichron Yaakov in northern Israel. She graduated from Givat Haviva Film School and also earned a bachelor's degree and teacher's certification from the David Yellin College of Education in Jerusalem. In 2003 she founded Ibtisam Films to produce documentaries that explore the boundaries of Palestinian and Israeli societies with a focus on women and minorities. Her film *77 Steps*, released in 2010, chronicles her love story with Yonatan, a Jew from Canada who was her neighbor in the Tel Aviv apartment building where she lived after moving from her village. Their three-year relationship took place without the knowledge of their families and was fraught with difficulties that ultimately led to their separation. In one scene from *77 Steps*, for example, Yonatan plans to celebrate Israel's Independence Day while she intends to commemorate the Palestinian Nakba Day.[3] "I understand where you come from," he tells her. "I understand the limits of our relationship." Looking back on this love affair, she admits that it was hard "to hide all the time" and "not to be able to talk about your love and share it because of this national difference."[4]

By revealing her love story in *77 Steps* (so named after the number of steps leading to her mother's house), Mara'ana tackled the issues of identity and intimate Jewish-Arab relationships. In her view, the subject of mixed Jewish-Arab couples is still socially and politically taboo in Israel. Describing the prevailing attitudes toward this question as "very primitive," she remarks: "We are in this world where we talk about development, we chase technological progress, but racially we are completely divided—it's bizarre."[5]

In an interview with the Portuguese journalist Margarida Santos Lopes, Mara'ana recounts that one of her biggest fears in making *77 Steps* was how Arab society would accept it. "To convince myself and in order to feel safe, I made a 'safe answer' to throw at anyone attacking me for exposing my relationship with a Jewish man. This 'safe answer' was that if Mahmoud Darwish could write love poems about his Jewish beloved (one of the poems is 'Rita and the Rifle'), it is perfectly fine that I'll make a movie about my relationship with my Jewish boyfriend—a controversial act in both Arab and Jewish societies in Israel. After the movie production ended, I went to seek who Rita is. I spent half a year doing research in which I found who Rita might be in Darwish's poetry. The name of that woman is Tamar Ben-Ami, and I found her living in Berlin. She revealed her love story with Mahmoud Darwish forty years ago. She also revealed love letters that Mahmoud sent her. That was when I understood that only through such a love story I can tell the story of a national poet."[6] In actual fact, Rita's identity was already well known in the Israeli press when Mara'ana went looking for her. The journalist Yehuda Atlas, for example, interviewed Tamar Ben-Ami in 1988 and reported the story of her relationship with Darwish (and the love letters he wrote her) in a detailed article titled "Shelakh, Mahmoud" that he published in the leading daily newspaper *Yediot Ahronot*.[7]

Not surprisingly, *77 Steps* provoked angry reactions among Palestinian Arabs, especially Palestinian women. "There is an accepted stereotype of an Arab man in love with a Jewish woman—it works," says Mara'ana, but the very idea of a Palestinian woman talking openly on a film about intimate relationships is a taboo. When it comes to mixed relationships, "a man can do it; he is entitled to."[8]

Today, Mara'ana is married to an Israeli Jew named Boaz Menuhin. They married in Tel Aviv in a nonreligious alternative ceremony that is not formally recognized by the state, where family law is governed by the authorities of a citizen's religion. Mara'ana-Menuhin states that their union has not been free of difficulties, but they have gained their families' approval. She acknowledges that dating a Jewish man was easier the second time around, not because her mother was less opposed to the idea itself, but because she was pleased that her daughter was finally getting married. She remembers her wedding as a surreal experience: "I was asking myself: 'What are they—our families, our friends—all doing here together? How did we manage to beat the system, and the hate, and the stereotypes?'"[9]

Unlike the happy ending of Mara'ana-Menuhin's love story, Mahmoud Darwish's experience of "love across boundaries" is a classic story of unrequited love. The poem "Rita and the Gun" (also known as "Rita and the Rifle"), set to music and sung by the Arab-Israeli singer Mira Awad (herself also married to an Israeli Jew), plays in the background of the opening scene in the documentary film, *Write Down, I Am an Arab*, expressing the young Darwish's longing for his beloved and his sorrow at their separation, while the voice of the older Darwish is heard telling Helit Yeshurun, editor of the Hebrew poetry magazine *Hadarim*, in a landmark interview conducted in 1996: "They say that every love poem of mine is about the land. That 'Rita' in *Eleven Planets* is Palestine. 'Rita' is an erotic poem, but no one believes me. ... Rita is a pseudonym, but it alludes to a particular woman. ... Rita in my poems is a Jewish woman. Is that a secret? A secret that I am revealing?"[10]

Darwish and Tamar Ben-Ami, alias Rita, met in the early 1960s. At the time, he was living and working in Haifa, which was a center of activity for Palestinian political and cultural leaders. In Haifa he joined the Israeli Communist Party and worked for its Arabic newspapers, *al-Jadid* and *al-Ittihad*, where he met Palestinian leaders such as Emile Touma, Tawfiq Toubi, and Emile Habibi. The Israeli Communist Party (known by the Hebrew acronym Maki and later Rakah) embraced Darwish, helped him develop his literary skills, and propelled him forward politically and nationally.[11]

Tamar Ben-Ami, née Berkman, was born in 1947 to Eastern European Jews from Poland and Russia who immigrated to Mandatory Palestine in the 1930s, thus escaping the Holocaust. Ben-Ami grew up in a middle-class neighborhood called Nave Sha'anan in Haifa. Her mother was a nurse at Rambam Hospital and her father worked as a clerk at the Income Tax Office in Haifa. Known as ardent supporters of the Israeli Communist Party, the parents instilled in their two daughters communist ideals, emphasizing the value of labor, the principle of solidarity among the world's working classes, and the importance of Arab-Jewish brotherhood. When Ben-Ami was in her teens, they sent her to a youth movement called Banki,[12] an acronym for the Israeli Communist Youth Alliance, which included both Jewish and Arab groups. Though organized separately because of the language barrier, the two groups had many joint activities, from going to the movies to trips and summer camps. Real ties of friendship did not develop between members of the two groups, but there was a sense of willingness, openness, and expectation that something like this would happen. In communist circles in Haifa at the time there were some notable examples of mixed Arab-Jewish couples: Saliva Khamis and Arna Mer, George and Tziporah Toubi, and Emile and Haya Touma, in whose house Darwish came to live. Haya was the choreographer of the dance delegation sent by the Israeli Communist Youth Alliance to the Democratic Youth festival in Helsinki, in which Ben-Ami participated, and hence the connection that eventually led to a meeting between Darwish and Ben-Ami.[13]

According to the journalist Yehuda Atlas, "It was Mahmoud who asked about her first, at Haya and Emile Touma's house, where he lived. She was then sixteen and a half years old, a high school student, active in the Israeli Communist Youth Alliance, known to be a dancer. He was twenty-two years old, editor of *al-Jadid*, the literary organ of Rakah, which came out in Haifa; a lyrical poet of Arabic, then in a transitional stage to Palestinian national poetry."[14]

They saw each other first at a political rally of the Israeli Communist Party organized in Shfaram, an Arab city (12 mi) east of Haifa, where a mixed troupe of Jewish and Arab dancers gave a performance. As Ben-Ami recounts, Darwish appeared first and recited two of his poems, after which he sat down in the first row and the dance troupe got on stage. As she was dancing, they exchanged glances, and sparks flew at that moment.[15]

By Yehuda Atlas's account, "Darwish saw her dancing; she heard him reading his poetry. She didn't understand it—the Jewish-Arab solidarity of the communist movement did not require the study of Arabic among the Jewish members—but she could feel the rhythm, the beat, the melody, the truth. He was also a handsome young man, blue-eyed, slim, always elegantly dressed, sensitive, ascetic, carrying his personal pain and the collective Palestinian pain."[16]

Ben-Ami was a pretty girl with a warm smile, fair-skin, hazel eyes, and long chestnut-colored hair. The romance that blossomed between the two of them is chronicled in the numerous love letters that Darwish wrote her and the photographs that they took together. Many of these letters, which Ben-Ami has kept to this day, are presented in Mara'ana-Menuhin's documentary film *Write Down, I Am an Arab*. Darwish's letters, professing his love, longing, and devotion to Ben-Ami, are written in fluent Hebrew and are laced with poetic images. They always begin with the word "Tamari," an endearing form of address meaning "My Tamar," and end with the words "Shelakh, Mahmoud," meaning, "Yours, Mahmoud." In one of these lyrical letters, he says, "Tamari, I am not writing; rather, I'm whispering in your ear. You are still with me. I hear your voice, I swim in the light of your eyes, I lean on your shoulder, I eat with you. I press your hand, which lies like a bird in my hand, a bird which has no desire to fly. Where will it go? From me ... to me. Yours, Mahmoud."[17] The resonant voice of the Arab-Israeli actor Makram Khoury is heard reciting several of these love letters as the documentary film artfully reconstructs Darwish's words and actions. In the released photographs, the young couple appears smiling happily, standing side by side, with Darwish's arm wrapped around Ben-Ami's shoulder, or Ben-Ami leaning affectionately against him, a bouquet of wildflowers in her hands. An air of bliss and innocence radiates from their beaming faces.

It was first love for both of them, enough to confuse any two young people even without the Arab-Jewish complication. Ben-Ami kept the true nature of their relationship secret, fearing the reactions of her social environment. On the one hand, she was proud that she had defied the social conventions and dared to have an Arab boyfriend, even feeling a sense of "stolen water is sweet," that is, forbidden delights are exciting and pleasant. On the other hand, she was a young and vulnerable girl, frightened by her own audacity to violate a major social taboo, afraid to go all the way and commit to him. She introduced Darwish to her parents as a friend, and as such he was welcome in their home. They knew who he was because they too attended the rallies of the Israeli Communist Party, at which both Alexander Penn, the renowned Jewish poet, and Darwish would recite from their respective poems. Ben-Ami and Darwish used to meet in his office in Wadi Nisnas, or at his place in the Toumas' house on Abbas Street, or in the apartment that he had later rented. She accompanied him when he was invited to read from his poetry before Arab audiences. She also visited his village of al-Jadida on the occasion of his brother's wedding and met his family, who received her cordially.[18]

Ben-Ami acknowledges that the Israeli Communist Youth Alliance not only brought her and Darwish together but also introduced her to the works of some of the world's greatest poets and intellectuals. There she learned about Pablo Neruda, Federico Garcia Lorca, Nazim Hikmet, Vladimir Mayakovski, Julian Tuwim, and Alexander Penn. Their poems, some of which she had learned by heart, provided her and Darwish with fodder for discussion. He would analyze their poems with her and talk about poetry. He would also translate his own poems into Hebrew for her.

The strong connection of his poems to the land, its soil, and its landscape moved her so deeply that years later it would inspire her creative work as a dancer and a choreographer.[19]

After graduating from high school, Ben-Ami deferred her army service so she could attend the Rubin Academy of Music and Dance in Jerusalem. The distance from Haifa made it difficult for the secret lovers to meet. The Arab population in Israel was under military administration at the time, and Darwish needed a permit to travel to Jerusalem, which he was often denied. Ben-Ami would return to Haifa for a visit once every fortnight. The anguish of their separation is echoed in Darwish's letters to her, which are full of longing and anticipation of her next visit. On one of these visits, they went to see the dancer Roni Segal and stayed with her till late at night, thereby missing the last bus back to Ben-Ami's house in Nave Sha'anan, so Darwish invited her to spend the night at his place. The next morning, when her parents discovered her whereabouts and the true nature of her relationship with Darwish, a scandal broke out. Feeling guilty for being the cause of her troubles at home, Darwish sent her an apologetic letter, expressing his deep regret for her suffering and assuring her that she was not alone; he was by her side. He wrote that he wanted to come to Jerusalem immediately to console her, but his request for a travel permit was denied by the military governor.[20]

It was not the first time that Darwish was denied a travel permit. He clashed repeatedly with the Israeli authorities because of his political poetry. His first arrest was in 1961, about a year after he had graduated from high school in Kafr Yasif and moved to Haifa. His second arrest, in 1965, was for traveling to Jerusalem without a permit to participate in a poetry reading organized in his honor by the Arab Students' Union in Jerusalem. In 1966 he was arrested for the third time on suspicion of hostile activity. His fourth arrest happened in 1967, five days after the outbreak of the Six-Day War, and in 1969 he was arrested for the fifth time. In addition, he had also spent time under house arrest.[21]

When Darwish was arrested presumably for the third time, he sent Ben-Ami a letter in which he urged her to come to Haifa at once to see him before he went to prison, emphasizing that there was no time for her to reply to him in writing and imploring her not to disappoint him.[22] Ben-Ami's response, real or imaginary, is depicted in Darwish's memoir, *Journal of an Ordinary Grief* (*Yawmiyyat al-huzn al-'adi*),[23] which came out in Beirut in 1973. Reminiscing about their love affair, he says:

I used to call her by a borrowed name because that is more beautiful. When I kissed her I was so full of desire between one kiss and another that I felt I would lose her if we stopped kissing.

Between sand and water she said, "I love you."

And between desire and torture I said, "I love you."

And when the officer asked what she was doing here, she answered, "Who are you?" And he said, "And who are you?"

She said, "I'm his sweetheart, you bastard, and I've come with him all the way to the gate of this prison to say goodbye. What do you want with him?"

He said, "You should know that I'm an officer."

"I too will be an officer next year," she said.

She brought out her military induction papers. The officer then smiled, and pulled me away to prison.

The following year the [1967] war erupted, and I was put in prison again. I thought of her: "What is she doing now?" She may be in Nablus, or another city, carrying a light rifle as one of the conquerors, and perhaps at this moment giving orders to some men to raise their arms or kneel on the ground. Or perhaps she is in charge of the interrogation and torture of an Arab girl her age, and as beautiful as she used to be.

She didn't say goodbye. (pp. 51–52)

Ben-Ami acknowledges that in Jerusalem the physical distance from Darwish ultimately created an emotional distance. She was busy with her school work, her dance troupe, and her Jewish friends, and driven by the desire to belong to the larger whole. She started drifting away from Darwish. In the end, despite her cosmopolitan outlook and deep feelings for him, she could not commit to him. "I blame myself for the separation," she candidly admits. "I wasn't strong enough to confront the hardships."[24] Sensing the change in her attitude, Darwish sent her pleading letters that are poignant examples of unrequited love. In one of them, he attributes her detachment to her being preoccupied with difficult thoughts that defy clarity. Referring to these thoughts as the "stormy sea" that she cannot overcome, he implores her not to make a final decision about their relationship now but to "rely on time and the wind to steer their ship" as they see fit. In a postscript, he adds that he started writing a long poem about them and that it was an arduous task.[25] As it happened, Darwish went on to write more than one poem about their love story. His suggestion to "rely on time and the wind to steer their ship" alludes to a famous verse by the medieval Arab poet al-Mutanabbi: "Not every human desire can be fulfilled / Winds may blow opposite to ships' wishes." In a subsequent letter, he sounds more desperate, confessing that he feels badly wounded, and sometimes quite pathetic, that he is unable to stop thinking of her, and that he can only see the "criminal" in her (i.e., the cruel side of her personality) rather than the sweet, beautiful aspects. He concludes this letter by apologizing for any insult his words might have caused, saying that he merely opened his heart for a brief moment, and was already closing it up.[26]

The breakup of their relationship appears to have been harder on Darwish than on Ben-Ami, who was drafted into the IDF shortly after the Six-Day War. She did not carry a rifle as one of the conquerors, as Darwish had imagined in his memoir *Journal of an Ordinary Grief*, nor did she give orders to some Arab men to kneel on the ground, nor was she in charge of the interrogation and torture of an Arab girl her age. As a graduate of the Rubin Academy of Music and Dance, she served in a naval troupe that entertained the troops with performances. "It was a wonderful time," she says, looking back with fondness.[27]

Subsequently, Darwish threw himself into poetry. Between 1960, the year he moved to Haifa, and 1970, the year he left Israel and went into self-exile, he published eight books of poetry, among them the famous poems "Identity Card" (1964), "To My Mother" (1966), "A Lover from Palestine" (1966), and "Rita and the Gun" (1968). In the landmark interview with Helit Yeshurun in 1996, he recounts that he wrote "To My Mother" while he was in prison. She came to visit him, bringing him coffee and fruit. He was touched by this gesture, for he got the idea into his head that his mother hated him because he was the middle child and because she used to hit him when he was a little boy. Realizing that he was wrong, he wrote her this personal poem through which he wanted to atone for the fallacious assumption he had held about her. He did not expect it to be set to music and to be sung by millions of Arabs; nor did he imagine that people would interpret this confessional poem as a poem of national longing and think that his mother was the homeland. "It was a letter of reconciliation from a child to his mother," he said quite simply in the interview.[28]

In early 1970 Darwish was sent by the Israeli Communist Party to study in Moscow. After spending a year there, he decided not to return to Israel, arriving instead in Cairo in February 1971. His departure provoked sharp criticism among Palestinians and across the Arab world, as it was seen as a betrayal of his role as the poet of the national resistance. Darwish gave three reasons for his departure: first, the oppressive conditions under which he was living in Israel, where he was trapped in Haifa and subject to repeated arrests and imprisonment, which had a stunting effect on his creativity and ability to contribute to the Palestinian cause; second, his desire for personal and professional growth, which would enable him to better serve the Palestinian cause; third, the change in the policy of the Israeli Communist Party in 1969, which claimed that it was a party of Israeli patriots, thereby triggering an identity crisis in him.[29]

Muna Abu Eid distinguishes three important stages in Darwish's life and career between 1970, when he left Israel and went into self-exile, and 1996 when he returned to the homeland. His first stop was Cairo (1971), where he stayed for about a year, working at the *al-Ahram* daily newspaper in the company of great Egyptian writers such as Naguib Mahfouz, Tawfiq al-Hakim, and Yusuf Idris. He then moved to Beirut, where he joined the Palestine Liberation Organization (PLO) and became one of its key activists, editing the PLO Research Center's journal *Shu'un Filastiniyya* (Palestinian Affairs). He stayed in Beirut a decade (1972–1982) during which he produced prolific poetry marked by a mix of the political/collective and the personal/individual, until he had to leave this city too, when Israel and its Lebanese Christian (Maronite) allies succeeded in expelling the PLO from the country. After a short stay in Tunisia, he left for Paris, where he spent a relatively long period (1983–1995) and wrote the best of his poetry, with an increasing emphasis on the personal, as illustrated by the collections *Fewer Roses* (1986), *Eleven Planets* (1992), and *Why Did You Leave the Horse Alone?* (1995). Throughout the 1980s, Darwish served as a member of the PLO's Executive Committee and also played a central role in the drafting of the Palestinian Declaration of Independence in 1988. But he was opposed to the Oslo Accords and resigned in protest from his position in the PLO after it signed them in 1993.[30]

Darwish's personal life proved hard to balance with his professional life, as evident from the fact that he was twice married and divorced. In 1976 he married Rana Qabbani, the niece of the acclaimed Syrian poet Nizar Qabbani. She was eighteen years old and he was thirty-four. The marriage did not last and she left him after a few years, reportedly to pursue a doctorate degree at Cambridge University in England. In 1984 he married an Egyptian translator, Hayat Heeni, but that marriage did not last either and ended after a year. There were no children from either marriage. Acknowledging that he was attached to being alone, Darwish said, "I never wanted children, maybe I'm afraid of responsibility. I'd need more stability. I change my mind, places, styles of writing. The center of my life is my poetry. What helps my poetry, I do; what damages it I avoid."[31]

In 1988, following the outbreak of the first Intifada (1987–1993), Darwish wrote the controversial poem "Those Who Are Passing between Fleeting Words" ("'Abirun fi kalam 'abir"), in which he called on the Israelis: "Get out of our native land / Out of our seashore, out of our sea / Out of our wheat, out of our salt, out of our wound / Out of everything, and get out / Of the memories of memory / O you who are passing between passing words."[32] As he explained in an interview with the poet Muhammad Hamza Ghanayim in 1996, he wrote this poem out of anger after seeing on French television how Israeli soldiers were beating up Palestinian children.[33] The poem caused an uproar in Israeli society, where many intellectuals interpreted it as a call for the destruction of the State of Israel. Darwish was heavily criticized and condemned in the Israeli media, and even his left-wing friends attacked him, saying that he had crossed the line between revolutionary poetry and war-mongering. Yitzhak Shamir, then Israel's prime minister, quoted the poem with outrage in the Knesset, declaring that it revealed the PLO's true intentions toward Israel. In an effort to calm the storm, Darwish wrote a letter to the poet Samih al-Qasim, asserting that his poem was misinterpreted and that he was calling on the Israelis to leave the occupied territories (i.e., the West Bank, Gaza, and East Jerusalem, captured in the Six-Day War in 1967), not the whole country.[34] He was sensitive to what Israeli-Jewish intellectuals thought of him and didn't want them to judge his entire poetry on the basis of this one poem. Acknowledging that the poem was aesthetically weak in being too angry and direct, he decided not to include it in any of his volumes or collected works (*diwan*).[35]

Among the few people who came to his defense at the time was Tamar Ben-Ami. She was now in her early forties, a successful dancer and choreographer who had won many prizes in Israel, France, and Germany. She had pursued her passion for modern dance both at home and abroad. In 1971 she traveled to New York City to study at the famed Alvin Ailey American Dance Theater. Returning to Israel a year later, when her mother was diagnosed with cancer, she worked hard to establish herself in this art form. She danced in various ensembles, created choreographic works for the renowned Batsheva Dance Company, and also teamed up with the distinguished dancer Sally Anne Friedland to give performances and set up dance workshops around the country. In 1991 she joined the State Ballet School in Berlin, where she taught and choreographed for nearly two decades, dividing her time between Tel Aviv and Berlin.

When the Israeli press came down hard on Darwish, Ben-Ami felt the need to defend him. She appeared on Israeli television, saying that she knew him as a person and could not imagine the evil intentions attributed to him. The interviewer said to her, "You yourself experienced the impossible love of youth, the love between you and the poet Mahmoud Darwish." Ben-Ami responded, "The value of Arab-Jewish solidarity and coexistence had an emotional effect on me. It was important to me. And there is something about that impossible love that is beyond wars, and perhaps because of them at times."[36] Her television interview was reported in the Israeli daily newspapers.

Darwish, who resided in Paris at the time, got hold of these newspapers. He read Ben-Ami's defense of him, was moved by her support after all the years, and contacted her to thank her. They subsequently kept in touch and he invited her to visit him in Paris. Ben-Ami recounts that she was thrilled to receive his invitation. For years she had been reexamining their love story, trying to understand what had or hadn't happened and why, asking herself whether she had disappointed him. "Sometimes I walk around with the feeling that I have betrayed him," she said in an interview in 1988. "All that had transpired between us was more than twenty years ago. We were both very young then. We tried to do something that was beyond our power to accomplish, at least beyond my power. I didn't know, actually, what to do with this love, where to take it, how to protect it, if at all."[37] The more she thought about Darwish, the more she longed to see him, to talk about what had or hadn't occurred, to close the circle.[38] She found a little hotel in Paris and flew there. They had not set an exact date for their meeting and Darwish wasn't there when she arrived. She waited nearly two weeks, calling his apartment daily, only to receive no answer. Finally, his housekeeper answered and told her that he would be there the next day. She felt excited as she headed to the meeting, but became frantic when she arrived at his apartment building, realizing that it housed the PLO members. Looking back on their much-anticipated meeting, she sadly admits, "There was certain closeness between us, but that's it." Yasser Arafat, the PLO leader, had called Darwish in the middle of the meeting, and they spoke in Arabic, which Ben-Ami couldn't understand. When the meeting ended, Darwish said to her, "We'll meet again tomorrow." She returned to her hotel and called him the next day, only to hear him say that he couldn't see her again. She was in disbelief. She had come all the way to Paris and had waited nearly two weeks in her hotel to meet with him, expecting it would be more than just once. But he kept saying, "I can't meet you." When she pressed for an explanation, he became stressed out and said, "Forget about romance. Get off the cloud. Forget about romance!" He also said, "You're not my girlfriend!" and "So many years have gone by." Crushed, Ben-Ami found herself bursting into hot tears.[39]

Not much is known about Ben-Ami's personal life except that she never married. The fact that she responded to Darwish's invitation to visit him in Paris and had high expectations about their meeting suggests that she looked forward to the renewal of their love affair. She was in her early forties then and he was nearing fifty. Their romance had taken place more than two decades earlier. She was very young at the time and not strong enough to cope with the problems that their relationship entailed. Also, she wanted to pursue her aspiration to become a professional dancer and choreographer, an aspiration that required single-mindedness, hard work, and travel abroad. She had made her choice and left the man who loved her and composed poems for her. Now older, mature, and accomplished, she assumed that they would reunite and pick up where they had left off, that this was his intention too in inviting her to come. But she was bitterly rebuffed. The man Darwish was in his early twenties was gone. He was now an internationally acclaimed poet and a cultural icon for millions of Arabs. As the voice of the Palestinian people and a member of the PLO Executive Committee, he had a public image to maintain and multiple political obligations to meet. He was not available, or perhaps not interested, in reviving an old romantic relationship, however pivotal it had been in his life. Was he a prisoner of the Palestinian political agenda, unable to balance his personal desires against his public obligations, or was he a sober, realistic man who had overcome the unrequited love of his youth and moved on, refusing to be trapped in the past? In the landmark interview with Helit Yeshurun in 1996, he said, "You can't return to be the same person that you once were, and you can't return to the same place as it once was—that's impossible."[40]

Darwish expressed similar sentiments about another romantic relationship in which the "other" was the beloved. As it happened, following the breakup with Ben-Ami, he had a love affair with another Israeli-Jewish woman whom he identified by the Hebrew name Shulamit (abbreviated as Shula) and to whom he dedicated a long love poem titled "Writing in the Light of a Rifle" ("Kitaba 'ala daw' bunduqiyya").[41] When asked about her in an interview for the *New York Times* conducted by the journalist Adam

Shatz in 2001, he said briefly: "We met after the 1967 war, and she was my last love in the country. I shouldn't say who she is, because she is still alive, and there is no returning to the past. Things and human beings have changed."[42]

Arab scholars have generally been reluctant to acknowledge that the Palestinian national poet had been passionately in love with an Israeli-Jewish woman. The story was largely shrouded in silence and mystery, at times distorted, and at other times interpreted metaphorically. Abdullah al-Shahham, for example, cites a "testimony" by A. Yaghi, who claims that "Rita was a soldier in the Israel Defense Forces, and Darwish truly loved her. They lived together for more than a short while—for two years. He did not hesitate to separate from her, due to their ideological differences. She was a Zionist extremist, and he was a sensitive poet who disliked Zionism and extremism."[43] This politically loaded statement is clearly intended to protect Darwish's image as the poet of the Palestinian national resistance. Rajaa al-Naqqash suggests that the love poem "Rita and the Gun" should be read metaphorically rather than literally: "In this way love falls apart under the assault of Zionist aggression, which is symbolized by the gun in this poem. It is not only a story of two lovers whose love is destroyed by the gun. The love itself is a symbol of the life and peace that could fill the land of Palestine and unite Muslims, Christians, and Jews, and the Arab lover and his Jewish beloved Rita, were it not for racism and neo-Nazism, were it not for Zionism, which is based on aggression, expansionism, and deep hatred of the Arabs."[44] Aside from bearing the stamp of political polemics, the suggestion that the unrequited love depicted in "Rita and the Gun" is merely a poetic metaphor, a fictional tale rather than a true story, is simply invalidated by the evidence presented in Mara'ana-Menuhin's documentary film, by the love letters that Darwish wrote to Ben-Ami, and by Darwish's own statements in many interviews. "'Rita' is indeed a true story, one that left a deep emotional scar," he confirmed, dismissing readers' attempts to interpret Rita as a metaphor for Palestine or love for the homeland.[45]

The reactions in Israeli society to the documentary film *Write Down, I Am an Arab* and the revelation of the love affair between Darwish and Ben-Ami were mixed. The fact that it won the Audience Choice Award when it premiered at Tel Aviv's DocAviv film festival in May 2014 indicates that it was viewed with empathy. But there were also angry voices that sharply denounced it, castigating Ben-Ami as a traitor and a disgrace to the Jewish people.[46] Darwish's figure and poetry were at the center of the public debate over the documentary film. Those who saw him as a representative

3 SELF-DEFINING MEMORIES: WHEN MAHMOUD MET "RITA" 59

of the enemy opposed the film and criticized the affair, and those who called for Arab-Jewish understanding viewed the film and the affair positively.[47] It is worth mentioning that in 2000, Israel's minister of education, Yossi Sarid, attempted to introduce a few of Darwish's poems into the required high school literature curriculum. It led to a stormy debate in the Knesset, and the government narrowly survived a no-confidence vote.

Following the signing of the Oslo Accords in 1993, Darwish's exile ended. Carrying a Palestinian identity card, he arrived in Israel on a three-day visit. In 1996, he returned to the land, dividing his time between Amman, Jordan, and Ramallah, the de facto Palestinian capital on the West Bank. Devoting himself to literature, he worked as director of the Palestine Literary Institute and as editor-in-chief of its journal, *al-Karmel*. He continued to write lyrical poetry, with bold historical allegories of the Palestinian experience and a reliance on myth and metaphysics, and to foster all aspects of Palestinian culture and heritage. He died on 9 August 2008, at the age of sixty-seven, in Houston, Texas, following heart surgery, and was given a state funeral in Ramallah, where he was laid to rest. As for Ben-Ami, in 2011, after a long and distinguished career at the State Ballet School in Berlin, where she worked as a teacher and a choreographer for nearly two decades, she retired. She was nearing seventy when she appeared in Mara'ana-Menuhin's documentary film *Write Down, I Am an Arab*, still carrying a torch for Darwish and preserving all his love letters. The film shows her visiting his grave on the anniversary of his death and laying a bouquet of red roses on his tombstone.

Long after it ended, Darwish and Ben-Ami's love story continued to maintain a powerful, bittersweet hold over their psyches. Ben-Ami describes her art and her entire personal life as being shaped by her time with Darwish.[48] Darwish went on to compose love poems about her, disguising her identity under the pseudonym Rita. Over the years, Rita became a leitmotif in his poetry, appearing again and again, like a haunting dream or an obsession. Most probably, the primary reason for this lasting effect on them is that it was their first love, a fact that they had both confirmed in interviews. Psychologists have explored the notion of "first" experiences, suggesting that "part of why firsts affect us so powerfully is that they're seared into our psyches with a vividness and clarity that don't fade as other memories do."[49] People experience the most "firsts" during the early parts of their lives, when they are in their late teens and early twenties. First experiences are always loaded with intense emotional sensations that etch them deeply into memory, creating what is called "flashbulb memories," that is, detailed and vivid memories that are retained for a lifetime. Usually, such memories are associated with important autobiographical or historical events. Memories like our first kiss or first romantic relationship or first sexual encounter, or our first day of school or college engage all our senses simultaneously and are full of novelty, which is why they are so long-lasting. First love, whether requited or unrequited, can cast a shadow over later relationships, forging the lens through which one sees new romantic relationships. Many people never really get over their first loves.[50]

While this theory helps to understand the power of first love, it does not explain why people return to the same memories again and again, especially if these memories are unhappy. The psychologists Jefferson A. Singer and Peter Salovey have studied the role of memory in understanding personality and the development of the self. Focusing on what is *remembered* rather than what is *forgotten* (which is the conventional psychoanalytical approach to memory), they present a view of memory that places it as a central repository of major conflicts and themes for the individual: "Autobiographical memories may reveal repetitive affective patterns and themes that stamp an individual's most important concerns and unresolved issues. These memories, called self-defining memories, are identifiable by their affective intensity, vividness, and familiarity to the individual."[51] Arguing that much of what is of greatest importance about an individual may be learned from consciously selected recollections, they examine both negative and positive self-defining memories and elucidate the different functions they serve. Basically, "Individuals may repetitively recall unpleasant self-defining memories because they are still struggling to work through and resolve the conflict raised by the memory. Whether consciously or unconsciously, they return to these topics in memory in the interest of mastering them. Only by reviving the memories into consciousness do individuals avail themselves of an opportunity to recast the meaning of previous events or to re-imagine them in a way that is more palatable to their self-image."[52] Positive repetitive self-defining memories function as motivators and as agents of nostalgia, while negative repetitive self-defining memories have an adaptive significance: the unresolved conflict or issue evoked by the self-defining memory, however saddening or likely to torment, may at least be confronted and questioned, and through imagination, a different, more satisfying ending may be created.[53] Singer and Salovey draw on literary sources—drama, poetry, fiction, biography, and autobiography—to demonstrate how self-defining memories have played a major role in the creative evolution of writers in both self-understanding and the portrayal of characters in their works.

Darwish's first love was unrequited. He had to come to terms with this painful experience and resolve the issues raised by it. The recurring poems/memories about Rita speak of two lovers with contradictory commitments and aspirations who stand on opposite sides of the divide, cultural, political, national, religious, and ethnic. These poems/memories helped the poet understand the complications of their impossible love and the inevitability of their separation. They also facilitated his efforts to define his sense of self, sort out his major concerns, and set up future goals. "Repetition of a particular memory in consciousness," say Singer and Salovey, "has a great effect upon us, but when this memory revives other memories that further stimulate similar thoughts and feelings, the effect helps define the central themes of personality."[54] For Darwish, these central themes were his Palestinian identity, culture, and heritage, the loss of his homeland, and the national struggle to regain it.

NOTES

1. Alona Ferber, "When the Palestinian National Poet Fell in Love with a Jew." *Haaretz* (4 June 2014). https://www.haaretz.com. Accessed 12 August 2017.
2. Cited from Maya Weinberg, "*Write Down, I Am an Arab*," under "Comments." https://www.kanopy.com. Accessed 15 July 2017.
3. Nakba—"the Catastrophe"—the Palestinian term for the 1948 Arab defeat and the establishment of the State of Israel.
4. Cited from Ferber, "When the Palestinian National Poet Fell in Love with a Jew."
5. Ibid.
6. Cited from Margarida Santos Lopes, "Darwish through the Eyes of Three Women—One of Them His Jewish Lover." http://margaridasantoslopes. com. Accessed 10 September 2017.
7. See note 10 below for the reference to Yehuda Atlas's article.
8. Cited from Ferber, "When the Palestinian National Poet Fell in Love with a Jew."
9. Cited from ibid.
10. The following account of the love affair between Darwish and "Rita" is based on multiple sources: Ibtisam Maraʿana-Menuhin's documentary film *Write Down, I Am an Arab* (*Sajjil ana ʿArabi*) (Tel Aviv: Ibtisam Films, 2014); articles published in leading Israeli newspapers, especially Yehuda Atlas's "Shelakh, Mahmoud" (Yours, Mahmoud), *Yediot Ahronot*, 7 days (25 March 1988), pp. 42–44; Muna Abu Eid, *Mahmoud Darwish: Literature and the Politics of Palestinian Identity* (London: I. B. Taurus, 2016);

and interviews with Mahmoud Darwish, especially the landmark 1996 interview in Hebrew conducted by Helit Yeshurun in *Hadarim: Magazine for Poetry* 12 (Spring 1996): 172–198. An abridged version of this landmark interview, translated by Adam Yale Stern, was published under the title "Exile Is So Strong Within Me, I May Bring It to the Land," *Journal of Palestine Studies* 42, no. 1 (Autumn 2012): 46–70. The present citation is from pp. 55, 56 of the translated interview.

11. Abu Eid, *Mahmoud Darwish*, p. 28.
12. Banki (Hebrew) stands for "Brit No'ar Komunisti Yisraeli," which means: Israeli Communist Youth Alliance.
13. Atlas, "Shelakh, Mahmoud," p. 42.
14. Ibid. Translation mine.
15. Ben-Ami, in Mara'ana-Menuhin, *Write Down, I Am an Arab*.
16. Atlas, "Shelakh, Mahmoud," p. 42. Translation mine.
17. This letter is quoted verbatim in Atlas, "Shelakh, Mahmoud," p. 43. Translation mine. The letter is also recited verbatim in Mara'ana-Menuhin, *Write Down, I Am an Arab*.
18. Atlas, "Shelakh, Mahmoud," p. 43.
19. Ibid., pp. 43, 44.
20. This letter is recited verbatim in Mara'ana-Menuhin, *Write Down, I Am an Arab*.
21. Abu Eid, *Mahmoud Darwish*, pp. 31–32.
22. This letter is recited verbatim in Mara'ana-Menuhin, *Write Down, I Am an Arab*. It is also mentioned in Atlas, "Shelakh, Mahmoud," p. 43.
23. Mahmoud Darwish, *Journal of an Ordinary Grief*, trans. Ibrahim Muhawi (Brooklyn: Archipelago Books, 2010). All citations are from this source.
24. Ben-Ami, in Mara'ana-Menuhin, *Write Down, I Am an Arab*.
25. This letter is recited verbatim in ibid.
26. This letter is recited verbatim in ibid.
27. Ben-Ami, in Mara'ana-Menuhin, *Write Down, I Am an Arab*.
28. Darwish, "Exile Is So Strong Within Me," p. 48.
29. Abu Eid, *Mahmoud Darwish*, pp. 34–36.
30. Ibid., pp. 37–43.
31. Cited in Maya Jaggi, "Poet of the Arab World: Mahmoud Darwish." *The Guardian* (7 June 2002), p. 5. www.theguardian.com/books. Accessed 16 August 2016.
32. This poem is translated by Kamal Abdel-Malek in *The Rhetoric of Violence: Arab-Jewish Encounters in Contemporary Palestinian Literature and Film* (New York: Palgrave Macmillan, 2005), pp. 154–155. This citation is reproduced with permission of Springer Nature Service Center.
33. Abu Eid, *Mahmoud Darwish*, pp. 141–142.
34. Ibid., p. 141.

35. Cited from "A Love Story between an Arab Poet and His Land," an interview with Mahmoud Darwish by Adam Shatz, *Journal of Palestine Studies* 31, no. 3 (Spring 2002), p. 71. See also Adam Shatz, "A Poet's Palestine as a Metaphor." *The New York Times* (22 December 2001), p. 3. http://www.nytimes.com. Accessed 16 August 2016; and Jaggi, "Poet of the Arab World," p. 6.

36. A clip from Ben-Ami's television interview is presented in Mara'ana-Menuhin, *Write Down, I Am an Arab*. Cited from this source.

37. Cited from Atlas, "Shelakh, Mahmoud," p. 44. Translation mine.

38. Cited from ibid.

39. Ben-Ami, in Mara'ana-Menuhin, *Write Down, I Am an Arab*.

40. Darwish, "Hagalut kol kach hazaka betochi," p. 1. Translation mine. This segment is not included in the abridged English translation of his interview published in *Journal of Palestine Studies* 42, no. 1 (Autumn 2012): 46–70.

41. The poem "Writing in the Light of a Rifle" ("Kitaba 'ala daw' bunduqiyya") was first published in the newspaper *Al-Jadid* in 1969, and later in Darwish's collection *My Beloved Rises from Her Sleep*, 1970; reprinted in Darwish, *Al-Diwan: al-a'mal al-ula*, 1: 346–355.

42. Cited from "A Love Story between an Arab Poet and His Land," an interview with Mahmoud Darwish, p. 73.

43. Abdullah al-Shahham, "A Portrait of the Israeli Woman as the Beloved: The Woman Soldier in the Poetry of Mahmud Darwish after the 1967 War," *Bulletin (British Society for Middle Eastern Studies)* 15, no. 1–2 (1988): 37. This "testimony" is also cited in Abdel-Malek, *The Rhetoric of Violence*, p. 70.

44. Raja' al-Naqqash, *Mahmud Darwish: sha'ir al-ard al-muhtalla* (Beirut: Dar al-Hilal, 1971), p. 206. Translation mine.

45. Abu Eid, *Mahmoud Darwish*, pp. 120–121.

46. See, for example, Rogel Alpher, "One Should Spit on the Terrorist Film *Write Down, I Am an Arab*, Which Incites to Kill the Jewish People" (in Hebrew). *Haaretz* (22 July 2016). https://www.haaretz.co.il. Accessed 12 August 2016.

47. See, for example, Gili Izikovich, "Mahmoud Darwish: 'Fuel for Terrorism' or a Poet That Israelis Must Get to Know?" (in Hebrew). *Haaretz* (20 July 2016). https://www.haaretz.co.il. Accessed 12 August 2016.

48. Cited in Mira Sucharov, "Are Love and Politics Mutually Exclusive in Israeli-Palestinian Conflict?" *Haaretz* (10 July 2015). https://www.haaretz.com. Accessed 26 July 2016.

49. Jay Dixit, "Heartbreaks and Home Runs: The Power of First Experiences." *Psychology Today* (1 January 2010). www.psychologytoday.com/articles. Accessed 30 August 2016.

50. Ellen McCarthy, "Why We Never Really Get over That First Love." *The Washington Post* (12 February 2016). https://www.washingtonpost.com. Accessed 3 August 2016.
51. Jefferson A. Singer and Peter Salovey, *The Remembered Self: Emotion and Memory in Personality* (New York: The Free Press, 1993), p. 4.
52. Ibid., pp. 40–41.
53. Ibid., pp. 36, 40–41, 43–44.
54. Ibid., p. 36.

CHAPTER 4

The Rita Love Poems and Prose Passages

Abstract This chapter offers a close reading of the love poems and prose passages that Darwish dedicated to Rita over a period of twenty-five years, from 1967 to 1992. I discuss dominant themes, images, and messages. I draw a comparison between the impossible love of Darwish and Rita and that of other famous lovers in literature, the Arab Qais and Layla and the European Romeo and Juliet, all of whom belonged to hostile/warring groups. Finally, I offer an explanation as to why Rita ceased to appear in Darwish's poetry from the end of 1992 until his death in 2008.

Keywords Rita and the Gun—iconic love poem · Mahmoud Darwish—love poems for Rita—analysis and interpretation · Mahmoud Darwish—prose passages for Rita—analysis and interpretation · Star-crossed lovers in literature

"What's in a name?" says Juliet to Romeo. "That which we call a rose / By any other word would smell as sweet." This famous line from Shakespeare's play of star-crossed lovers is often used to imply that a name is an artificial and meaningless convention that does not affect or define what a person really is. Juliet argues that it is only Romeo's family name, Montague, which is her enemy, not he himself, and suggests that they both repudiate their family names and exist as unnamed selves. This provocative idea underlies

© The Author(s) 2019   65
D. Cohen-Mor, *Mahmoud Darwish*,
https://doi.org/10.1007/978-3-030-24162-9_4

66   D. COHEN-MOR

the central struggle and tragedy of the couple, who are doomed from the start as members of two warring families.[1]

In arguing that the name of the rose is arbitrary, Juliet makes a valid point, but in suggesting that Romeo can arbitrarily cease to be a Montague, she is naïve. It is impossible for people to repudiate the names that differentiate them, for they would still belong to their particular groups by indissoluble ties of family, history, and culture. Names are markers and a part of what we are. They identify not only who we are but also what our origins are—national, cultural, ethnic, and religious. Mahmoud Darwish's name locates him firmly within Arab-Muslim culture. Tamar Ben-Ami's name locates her firmly within Israeli-Jewish culture. Given the Arab-Israeli conflict, to be in love would be forbidden simply because of their identities, allegiances, and affiliations. In this situation, it is not surprising that he chose to use a pseudonym to refer to his Jewish lover. The name Rita, which is the short version of Margarita, is used in many languages around the world. It denotes the rare and precious globule found in nature inside the shell of an oyster—a pearl. Highly valued as a jewel, a pearl symbolizes the purity and beauty of its wearer.

The first appearance of Rita is in the poem "Rita and the Gun" (published in the collection *The End of the Night*, 1967). She returns again in the poems "Birds Die in Galilee" and "Rita, Love Me" (both published in the collection *Birds Die in Galilee*, 1969), then in the poem "The Sleeping Garden" (published in the collection *Weddings*, 1977), and finally in the poem "Rita's Winter" (published in the collection *Eleven Planets*, 1992). In addition, Rita appears in two prose works by Darwish: *Journal of an Ordinary Grief* (1973) and *Memory for Forgetfulness* (1982). These poems and prose passages abound in autobiographical elements: they tell the story of their love, their dreams and aspirations, their worries and isolation, and their painful separation. Although Darwish had not written an autobiography and kept his personal life private, his poems and prose works provide a fascinating window into intimate aspects of his life.

"Rita and the Gun" ("Rita wa-al-bunduqiyya," 1967) is the most famous of the love poems dedicated to Rita.[2] Set to music and sung by great performers such as the Lebanese Marcel Khalife and the Israeli-Arab Mira Awad, it achieved enormous popularity among adoring Arab audiences. The opening and concluding line of the poem is: "Between Rita and my eyes is a gun." This short statement establishes at once the reason for the lovers' separation: a deadly weapon, representative of war and violence. The poet recalls the dazzling beauty of his beloved's hazel eyes, which evoke associations with divinity in his mind. He nostalgically reminisces about their romance, how he kissed her and her lovely braids covered his arm, how they made pledges to each other and felt reborn in the passion of their love. Rita's name was "a feast" in his mouth and her body was "a wedding" in his blood. He recounts that they spent two years together during which they shared many tender moments, until that gun came between them. Although Rita has no voice in this erotic poem and is silent, her silence is imbued with sensuality. The lovers' separation is blamed on the armed conflict between their respective communities: first came the gun, which "fired on" them and destroyed their relationship, and then the city, which "swept Rita away." The gun represents the Israeli military, which is seen as an agent of aggression. The city, which is a recurrent image in Darwish's poetry, represents an oppressive society or country. The Arabic word for city, *madina*, is similar to the Hebrew word *medina*, which means "a state" and which is used to refer to the State of Israel (as in the expressions *ha-medina* and *medinat yisrael*).[3] The gun and the city suggest that Rita was drafted into the Israel Defense Forces (IDF), a situation that puts the lovers on opposite sides of the divide and terminates their relationship. The sorrowful poet bemoans the loss of his love as he recalls these vivid memories from the past.

Unlike the iconic poem "Rita and the Gun," which attributes the lovers' breakup to the objective reality of the ongoing Arab-Israeli conflict, the poem "Birds Die in Galilee" (1969) explains their breakup as stemming from a clash in their personal aspirations and connection to the land.[4] Here Rita has a voice and she speaks out. In the opening stanza, she promises her lover vaguely that they will meet again in the future, perhaps in a year or two or a generation, as she shoots with her camera pictures of gardens and the birds of Galilee. Then she departs to search beyond the sea for "a new meaning to truth." Arab critics have tended to interpret this line as Rita's disenchantment with the State of Israel and her decision to immigrate to another country free of Zionist ideology and war. But biographical information about Ben-Ami clearly refutes this interpretation and indicates that she traveled abroad to study modern dance—this art form was her avenue of authentic self-expression—and pursue a career as a professional dancer and choreographer. Her lover, however, regards her departure as an act of fleeing and cannot understand how she can abandon him and her country. He remains behind, deeply attached to the land, which, being under occupation, is depicted as "a clothes-line / for the handkerchiefs of blood / shed every minute."[5] In this poem, the lovers do not see eye to eye

68   D. COHEN-MOR

and their relationship is fraught with tension, a factor that precipitates the onset of emotional distancing and estrangement. The poet complains that nothing used to tire him at night but her silence; it pained and wounded him like an axe. Frustrated with his beloved's lack of commitment to him, he cynically calls on her to publicly renounce their love by joining in the killing that takes place outside the window of her house. In the last stanza, he realizes that his love for Rita is untenable and incompatible with his attachment to the land and its destiny. His public persona as "a lover from Palestine," namely, as a patriot, takes precedence over his personal feelings for Rita. Choosing to affirm his national identity and sense of belonging to the land, he says: "Rita / I am he in whose skin / The shackles etch / A likeness of the homeland."[6]

The third poem dedicated to Rita, poignantly titled "Rita, Love Me!" originally included the phrase "A Song Not Written by Mikis Theodorakis" above the title. This phrase was removed from subsequent printings of the poem in the volume *Birds Die in Galilee* (1969) and in Darwish's *diwan* (collected works).[7] However, the name of Mikis Theodorakis is crucial for understanding the inspiration for this poem and why it is set in the city of Athens in Greece. Born in the Greek island of Chios in 1925, Theodorakis is often referred to as Greece's most celebrated composer and songwriter who contributed to the cultural revolution in his country. He tenaciously opposed oppressive regimes, was imprisoned by the Greek junta of 1967–1974, and spent several years in exile in Paris (1970–1974), where he continued to fight against the colonels' dictatorship in his country. As part of his struggle for the restoration of democracy in Greece, he gave concert tours all over the world and became the symbol of resistance against the Greek dictatorship. In retaliation, the colonels' regime banned playing and listening to his music in Greece. After the fall of the junta in 1974, Theodorakis returned to his home country and, alongside his activities as a composer, played part in public life, serving as a member of parliament and as a government minister. He also continued to speak out in favor of left-liberal causes and Greek-Turkish-Cypriot friendly relations, and to be committed to raising international awareness of human rights and the need for peace.

Given this background information, it is easy to see why the poem "Rita, Love Me!" is set in Athens and why Theodorakis's name was originally mentioned above the title. Obviously, Darwish identified with the figure of this freedom fighter and saw similarities between the stories of their lives: both of them experienced arrests, imprisonment, and exile at the hands of the military authorities in their home countries, and both of them used their creative gifts, whether in composing music or composing poetry, as a medium of resistance in exile, be it internal or external. In Darwish's poem, the city of Athens is a thinly disguised allusion to the State of Israel. It is depicted as a site of oppression, where the police are ubiquitous and "every misery is appropriated" by them, where "love is forbidden," and where "grief has become the identity card" of the people.[8] The poet sees himself as a handcuffed prisoner dangling between the harsh political reality and a dream world of the imagination. In a refrain that is repeated several times, he pleads with his Jewish lover, "Rita, love me! and die in Athens / like the scent of jasmine / so the prisoner's desires may die."[9] Death for the sake of love will free him from his unfulfilled yearnings. Rita is absent and silent. The poet asserts that he experiences several forms of exile, physical, psychological, and emotional, as well as the estrangement of love, which he depicts as "a lover hanging her lover's garment / on the end of a cloud,"[10] a vivid image that alludes to the fleeting and fickle nature of love. He finds escape in a series of dreams in which erotic love merges with the land and he becomes engrossed in a search for his roots and the history of the land. In the final dream, he imagines that the city's repressive shackles dissolve through the revolutionary power of poetry, which brings change and renewal to the land, where now two lovers who come from opposite sides of the divide can "track down childhood," that is, experience the magic, spontaneity, and pleasure of a carefree romance.

While the image of the poet-speaker in the three poems discussed above is that of the abandoned, frustrated lover, in "The Sleeping Garden" (1977) Darwish assumes the reverse role of the lover who abandons his beloved. It is an agonizing act for him, for he has not ceased loving Rita, and her beauty, which he depicts as a luscious garden, continues to captivate him. To escape a painful confrontation—or perhaps to avoid a sudden feeling of remorse—he leaves her stealthily, while she is fast asleep, without even bidding her farewell. As he goes out of their room and steps outside, he sees the tree where she kissed him, and the recollection makes him hesitate momentarily, but then he continues to walk. "From now on I am estranged from my memories and my home," he says.[11] However, in his mind he immediately begins to replay detailed scenes from their relationship: how Rita wakes up in the morning and gets her kiss, how she brings him his Arab coffee and her *café au lait*, how she inquires about their love, and how he replies that he is at the mercy of the hands that bring him his coffee in the morning. "I love you Rita," he confesses several times.

70   D. COHEN-MOR

"I love you. Sleep while I leave."[12] No motive is provided for his departure: "Without a reason, like the birds of prey, I leave / Without a reason, like the ineffectual gust."[13] However, the line "Rita is asleep but her dreams are awake," which is repeated twice in the poem, suggests that her dreams may have something to do with his decision to leave. The dreams may allude to the ideology that Rita was brought up on, an ideology that would inspire her to serve in the Israeli army. Or the dreams may allude to her ambition to become a professional dancer, an ambition that would make her travel far away from the country. These dreams conflict with their love and are incompatible with the idea of sharing a future together. This realization might be the underlying motive for the poet's decision to part ways with his lover. The short exchange between them, which runs through his mind, reveals the hopelessness of their relationship. Rita asks, "Shall we get married?" He answers, "Yes." She asks, "When?" He replies, "When the violets grow / on the soldiers' helmets."[14] Just as it is impossible for flowers to sprout on the soldiers' helmets, so it is impossible for the two of them to get married—the odds are stacked against them. The poem concludes with the poet's departure amid repeated affirmations of his love for Rita and an admission that many winters from now he will wonder whether she is "still asleep or awake," that is, still escaping from reality or facing it.

After the separation depicted in "The Sleeping Garden," Rita disappears from Darwish's poems for "many winters," only to reappear in two of his prose works. The first one, *Journal of an Ordinary Grief* (*Yawmiyat al-huzn al-'adi*, 1973),[15] contains autobiographical essays that offer an intimate account of the complex existential realities of the Palestinians in Israel and reveal the ambiguity of Darwish's own identity as an Israeli Arab. In a recollection of presumably the third time that he was arrested and sentenced to prison, the poet talks about Rita. He depicts his encounter with her as love at first sight and says that he used to call her by an assumed name:

> She used to sing a lot, and I didn't understand her songs except in dreams. And she's beautiful! Beautiful! The moment I saw her, the clouds lifted from my mind. I snatched her away to my house and said, "Consider this love."
>
> She laughed. Even in the darkest hour she laughed.
>
> I used to call her by a borrowed name because that is more beautiful. When I kissed her I was so full of desire between one kiss and another that I felt I would lose her if we stopped kissing.

4 THE RITA LOVE POEMS AND PROSE PASSAGES   71

Between sand and water, she said, "I love you."

And between desire and torture, I said, "I love you."

And when the officer asked what she was doing here, she answered, "Who are you? And he said, "And who are you?"

She said, "I'm his sweetheart, you bastard, and I've come with him all the way to the gate of this prison to say goodbye. What do you want with him?"

He said, "You should know that I'm an officer."

"I too will be an officer next year," she said.

She brought out her military induction papers. The officer then smiled, and pulled me away to prison.

The following year, the [1967] war erupted, and I was put in prison again. I thought of her: "What is she doing now?" She may be in Nablus, or another city, carrying a light rifle as one of the conquerors, and perhaps at this moment giving orders to some men to raise their arms or kneel on the ground. Or perhaps she is in charge of the interrogation and torture of an Arab girl her age, and as beautiful as she used to be.

She didn't say goodbye.

And you didn't say: "Go, and come back."

You taught her to smoke, and she taught you the companionship of smoke. (pp. 51–52)

In this recollection, Rita appears as a feisty and lively girl who likes to sing and laugh, has tender feelings for Darwish, and defiantly escorts him to the gate of his prison. She is not afraid to confront the Israeli officer and tell him that she is his prisoner's sweetheart. But all this public display of affection and flouting of social norms comes to an end when she is drafted into the Israeli army. Becoming an IDF soldier shows that her primary commitment is to her people and her country, and that she chooses them over love. Darwish's nostalgic memories of her are mingled with pain and resentment: "She didn't say goodbye." Subsequently, her image transforms in his mind from a sweet and innocent girl whom he taught to smoke to an arrogant representative of the enemy who carries a rifle, orders Arab men to kneel on the ground, and brutally interrogates a young Arab girl. His final words, "You taught her to smoke, and she taught you the companionship of smoke," allude perhaps to the fleeting nature of her love, which did not last and vanished like smoke.

72 D. COHEN-MOR

The second work of prose in which Rita is evoked is *Memory for Forgetfulness* (*Dhakira lil-nisyan*, 1986).[16] The setting of this work is the 1982 Israeli invasion of Lebanon and the siege of Beirut, which Darwish had experienced firsthand. Recording a single day on the streets of the war-ravaged city, which provided a haven for the Palestinian Liberation Organization from the late 1960s until their expulsion in 1982, the poet reflects on the invasion and its political and historical dimensions. He ponders the meaning of exile, the role of the writer in a time of war, and the relationship of writing (memory) to history (forgetfulness), suggesting an intimate connection between writing, homeland, meaning, and resistance.

As he takes shelter from the air raid in a bar, Darwish finds himself musing about love and sexual desire. He recalls his Jewish lover and the intense passion of their forbidden love. Although she is not mentioned by name, several clues in the text suggest that he is referring to Rita. For one thing, her persona, as it comes across from the dialogue between them, is akin to that of Rita. For another, a certain wish that she expresses in this prose passage is later repeated in a slight variation in a new poem dedicated to Rita and bearing her name. The prose passage begins with the words: "'Take me to Australia,' she said. And I realized the time had come for us to get away from discord and war. 'Take me to Australia'—because I couldn't reach Jerusalem" (p. 121). The words "Take me to Australia" echo a similar line in the poem "Rita's Winter," which reads: "Take me to a faraway land, Rita sobbed, this winter / is long."[17] Her wish to escape the oppressive conditions of "discord and war" by fleeing to a faraway land—Australia—can't be fulfilled, just as the poet's wish to travel to Jerusalem can't be fulfilled.[18] The impossibility of either one of these courses of action suggests that the lovers are trapped.

The poet is astonished to find himself reminiscing about his Jewish lover in the midst of war. He asks himself:

> But why am I remembering her in this hell, and at this hour of the afternoon? And in this air-raid shelter of a bar? Is it because the woman sitting across from me is reenacting the screaming scene? Or is it because a dream brought her out of my dream at dawn? I don't know, exactly as I don't know why I remember my mother, the first lesson in reading, my first girl under the pine tree, and the riddle of the shepherd's pipe that has chased me for twenty-five years. The circle returns to its starting point.
>
> (*Each would kill the other outside the window.*) (pp. 121–122)

The last line (in italics and parentheses in the original), which is repeated each time the poet recalls his passion for his Jewish lover, is taken from Darwish's poem "A Beautiful Woman in Sodom" (published in the volume *Birds Die in Galilee*, 1969). The line implies that the romantic couple who makes love by the window would kill each other outside it because they are enemies, or alternatively, that their respective communities of Arabs and Jews are killing one another outside the window.[19]

Unlike the Rita poems discussed earlier, where the Jewish lover is usually silent and her personality is unveiled to the reader through the eyes of the poet, who describes what she looks like and how she acts, in this prose passage from *Memory for Forgetfulness* the Jewish lover takes part in a series of dialogues with the poet and her personality is revealed through her own voice and words. The setting is a room in a house where the couple has spent the night making love. It is raining outside, but the atmosphere inside is romantic, with logs burning in the fireplace and Leonard Cohen's song "Suzanne takes you down to her place by the river" playing in the background. The following line, in which the Jewish lover teases the poet to take his time with her, shows that she is witty and sensual: "Don't bite me like an apple; the whole night's still ours" (p. 122). Another exchange shows that she is full of mirth and energy:

"It's five in the morning, my dear."

"And does the Arab get sleepy?" she asked playfully. "As for me, I don't want to sleep."

I said, "Yes. The Arab does get sleepy, and tries to sleep."

She said, "Go ahead. I'll guard your sleep." (p. 124)

Hiding from the outside world in the cocoon of their room takes a toll on the Jewish lover. The words, "Take me to Australia," which she repeats three times in this long recollection, show that she is suffering from a sense of claustrophobia. She pleads with the poet to take her to a remote country "where there's no one belonging to you or me, not even you and me" (p. 122). At the same time, she is sensitive to what he thinks of her community, especially in light of his repeated arrests and imprisonment. "Do you hate Jews?" she cautiously asks. Evasively, the poet replies to her question with a question: "Do you love Arabs?" Although she presses on, he gives her no clear answer. The impossibility of their situation is not lost on either

74 D. COHEN-MOR

of them, and each, in turn, blames the other for being crazy: "I said, 'Are you crazy?' She said, 'A little'" (p. 124). Moments later, this dialogue is reversed, "She said, 'Are you crazy?' I said, 'A little'" (p. 125).

Because the world outside is full of strife, hostility, and violence, the lovers need to reassure themselves of their love for each other. In the following exchange, they are simultaneously flirting and jabbing each other:

> --Do you love me?
> --No. I don't love you. Did you know that your mother, Sarah, drove my mother, Hagar, into the desert?
> --Am I to blame then? Is it for that you don't love me?
> --No. You're not to blame; and because of that I don't love you. Or, I love you. My dear, my beautiful, my queen! (pp. 125–126)

The erotic element of their love is highlighted in this recollection and is depicted in lyrical terms: "Passion generated from passion. A rain that didn't stop. A fire that couldn't be put out. A body without end. A desire that lit up the bones and the darkness. We didn't sleep except to be awakened by the thirst of salt for honey and the smell of slightly burned coffee, roasting over burning marble. Cold and hot was this night. Hot and cold was that moaning" (p. 123). In fact, the erotic element runs throughout *Memory for Forgetfulness*, where it serves as a counterpart to death and is triggered by the instinct of self-survival in a time of war. Musing about people's heightened sexual activity amid the chaos of war, the poet rhetorically asks: "Is this a time for love? This is no time for love, but for sudden desire. Two fleeting bodies collaborate to hold back one fleeting death by means of another—a honeyed death" (p. 57). The expression "a honeyed death," which Darwish uses here for sex, is a variation on the French expression *la petite mort*—"the little death," which is popularly used as a euphemism for orgasm because of the brief loss or weakening of consciousness that follows it.

The present recollection ends on a somber note: the poet tells his Jewish lover that he must report to the Haifa police twice a day—or else risk another prison term. When the astonished lover asks what he will say in court to explain his absence, he replies:

> --I'll say I was here, reliving the Song of Songs.
> --Are you crazy?
> --Crazy.

4 THE RITA LOVE POEMS AND PROSE PASSAGES   75

--And you don't love me?
--I don't know.
And each is killing the other by the window. (p. 126)

There is a sense of desperation mingled with cynicism in the poet's reply. He is aware that the harsh political reality—"each is killing the other by the window"—persists and is unlikely to change in the near future. However long he and his Jewish lover may stay hunkered down in their room, they cannot escape the world outside. "The circle returns to its starting point" (p. 122), he notes as he recalls their love affair, tacitly acknowledging that it was inevitable that it should come to an end.

Fifteen years after featuring in the poem "The Sleeping Garden" (1977), Rita makes her final appearance in a poem by Darwish in "Rita's Winter" (1992). In this long poem, which comprises a series of stanzas and scenes, the lovers are alone on a bed in a small room atop a mountain. When Rita sleeps, the atmosphere is serene and intimate, but when she is awake, it becomes fraught with tension. In the exchange that takes place between the two of them, it is hard to tell "whether they are flirting or twisting the knife."[20] When Rita protests that she doesn't get the meaning of her lover's words, he replies, "Nor do I, my language is shrapnel."[21] Rita confesses that she has "left her mother" and defied the "city guards" in loving the poet. Surrounded by a hostile society, the couple is isolated: "I and you / are a little joy in a narrow bed ... a small joy / they haven't killed yet."[22] The social pressure takes its toll on them, and they feel lonely and beleaguered. "Take me to a faraway land, Rita sobbed, this winter / is long."[23] Although the poet is in a state of existential exile and cannot "find a horizon," he is not prepared to leave. The two lovers, "bewildered in unison on the bed," slowly become distant, "like a greeting between strangers on the pier."[24] Restless and eager to pursue her dreams, Rita gets up and ventures alone into the unknown, leaving her lover behind.

The poem can be interpreted both literally and figuratively. Taken in its literal sense, the poem depicts a strained relationship between two lovers who are wholly different in personality and outlook. The woman is pragmatic, concerned with her future and worldly matters. The man is an idealist, committed to his poetic and national mission. The two lovers represent "two dreams on the pillow, they intersect and escape so one / draws out a dagger and another entrusts the commandments to the flute."[25] In the poem's opening scene, the lovers are cuddled together on the bed; in the concluding scene, Rita places her handgun on her lover's draft poem and departs, having announced in advance: "I will return when the days and the dreams change."[26] The mention of the handgun calls to mind the line "Between Rita and my eyes is a gun" in the iconic poem "Rita and the Gun." The words "dagger" and "handgun" are associated with the woman, whereas the words "flute" and "draft poem" are associated with the man, thus signifying the ideological division between them. Taken in its figurative sense, the strained relationship of the couple in this poem is a metaphor for Arab-Jewish relations. Despite having a common ancestor—Abraham, and a common belief in a single God—monotheism, the two nations are locked in a relentless struggle. The contested land is likened to a small room atop a mountain overlooking the sea—it cannot hold two nations: "There is no land for two bodies in one, no exile for exile / in these small rooms, and exit is entry: / We sing between two chasms in vain."[27] These somber words capture the core of the Arab-Israeli conflict (or more precisely, the Israeli-Palestinian conflict), now persisting for over a century, with no end in sight.

"Rita's Winter" is the last poem dedicated to Rita, after which she disappears from Darwish's writings. It would seem that the poet was finally able to find closure to this tormenting love story and move on. What might have helped him find this belated closure? We know that this poem was published in 1992, long after his last meeting with Ben-Ami in Paris. It is possible that the face-to-face meeting with her after so many years had finally liberated him from the need to revisit their doomed love affair. Perhaps seeing her in the flesh and talking with her again had given him the opportunity to demonstrate to himself that he was different now, that desire had faded, and that circumstance itself had changed. The meeting might have disabused him of lingering nostalgic and romantic notions about her and might have resolved any residual issues pertaining to his self-definition and personal goals.[28] As evident from Ben-Ami's account, she came to this meeting with high expectations, anticipating that it would rekindle their love story.[29] But after meeting with her just once, Darwish rebuffed her, telling her on the telephone that she was no longer his girlfriend and that she should forget about romance. He was now an established poet with an international acclaim and a major political figure in the Palestinian Liberation Organization. The Oslo Accords, which he opposed, loomed ahead (they were signed in 1993). He had important political obligations to fulfill and more urgent topics to write about. Above all else, he always sought to achieve growth as a poet and strove hard to ensure that his poetry would continue to evolve in theme and style. Now that he had found closure, the Rita leitmotif had exhausted itself, and he was ready to explore new topics.

When reviewing all the Rita poems and prose passages, certain motifs stand out. Most conspicuous among them is the motif of sleep. In every one of the Rita poems, Rita is depicted as either asleep (denoting the state) or sleeping (denoting the action). For example, in "Rita's Winter" the opening line is "Rita sleeps in her body's garden" (p. 88). In "The Sleeping Garden" the line "Rita is asleep but her dreams are awake" (p. 160) is repeated twice. In "Rita and the Gun" the poet says, "And for two years she slept on my arm" (p. 51), and in "Rita, Love Me!" he says, "Sleep with my dream" (p. 80).[30] Sleep has many meanings, the most obvious of which is rest and healing: during sleep, one can relax the mind and body, allowing them to recover from experiences in wakeful life and feel peace and serenity. At the same time, sleep can signify an escape from reality, when one seeks an altered state of consciousness in order to forget a pressing problem or avoid facing a situation that is experienced as harsh and painful. The close connection between sleeping and dreaming is of paramount importance. Dreams can alter one's waking perception of reality, influence one's decisions, and inspire a particular course of action. For example, in "Rita, Love Me!" Darwish writes: "In the dream the dark eyes widen / the chains shiver / the night resigns / the poem is freed / in its earthy imagination" (p. 81). Frequently, dreams reveal important aspects of one's personality, serve as mirrors of reality, and foreshadow future events.[31]

It is fascinating to read Darwish's own thoughts on the topic of sleep in his third and final work of prose, *Absent Presence*, which he published near the end of his life, when he thought it might be his last work.[32] Partially autobiographical, the book explores the meaning of life, the impact of exile, and the nature of relationships, offering lyrical meditations on love, longing, Palestine, history, friendship, and family. Viewed as Darwish's self-elegy, the book depicts a life lived under the specter of death (he suffered from a heart condition). The title refers to those Palestinians, among them Darwish himself, who, after the 1948 Arab-Israeli war, made it back home too late for the first Israeli census and were classified as "present-absentees." In the following excerpt, Darwish enumerates the many blessings of sleep:

You love sleep, the unconscious wakefulness as you are now. Sleep is a lord, a sultan. Asleep, you are lord of yourself, sultan of yourself; alive without life's troubles; alive in a metaphorical death, selected in the care of angels, to train the body to visit the invisible with the manner fit for the suitable.

78   D. COHEN-MOR

The sleeper does not grow old in sleep; he does not fear, does not hear news which squeezes the bitter apple in the heart. ... Sleep is the high joy of forgetting, and if you dream, it is because the memory remembers obscure things it had forgotten. ... Sleep is the offering of whiteness to the sense, the exploration, without guides, fortune tellers or Sufis, of the limitless azure of sky and sea. Sleepers are equals despite the differences of beds and secrets. But waking divides sleepers and drags them to wars before and after sleep. If the world slept more, it would have fewer divisions. ... Sleep is the filling of the body with calm and peace of mind, the emptying of the mind of terror and grief. In sleep, there is no grief, no danger. (pp. 69–70)

At the same time, Darwish acknowledges the occurrence of nightmares in sleep and the close connection between sleep and death. He concludes his meditation on sleep with the remark, "Hypnos, the Greek god of sleep, revives you, and you forget that he is the brother of Death" (p. 72). Rhetorically, he asks, "Is death a long sleep, or is sleep a brief death?" (p. 73).

Other salient motifs in the Rita poems and prose passages are what the literary critic Subhi Hadidi calls the "inseparability of love and exile" and the "estrangement of love."[33] As he elaborates, it is a question of the fundamental duality of the lover and the beloved, who are strangers.[34] For example, in the poem "Rita, Love Me!" the poet says, "My exile: a lover hanging her lover's garment / on the end of a cloud,"[35] thus combining the theme of love with that of exile. The love encounter becomes at once the site of possibility and of discord and struggle. The lovers' quest for authentic identity and self-fulfillment may set them on different, separate paths, which can create a sense of alienation between them and ultimately lead to their separation. In the poem "Rita's Winter," for example, the poet depicts two lovers who are engaged in intimate relations but are slowly becoming estranged from each other: "the two of us bewildered in unison on the bed / before we became distant like a greeting between strangers on the pier / then departure carried us like a paper in its wind."[36] The lovers' separation takes place abruptly and without a farewell. In *Journal of an Ordinary Grief*, for example, the poet reminisces that when Rita left him, "she didn't say goodbye."[37] And in the poem "The Sleeping Garden" the situation is reversed and it is the poet who doesn't say goodbye, leaving Rita stealthily while she is fast asleep.

Intriguingly, in *Absent Presence*, Darwish writes that he actually prefers the end of a love affair to be swift and abrupt: "I do not want to see Romeo and Juliet, or Qais and Laila, in front of me at the low point of life. Love has an expiry date, like life or like tinned goods and medicines. I prefer it

4 THE RITA LOVE POEMS AND PROSE PASSAGES   79

that love should collapse, of heart failure, when lust and passion are at their height, as a horse falls from a mountain into an abyss."[38] While the tendency to compare Darwish and Rita to Romeo and Juliet is irresistible, there is a sharp contrast between these two couples: neither Darwish nor Rita was prepared to sacrifice everything for each other. Nor can Darwish and Rita be likened to the seventh-century Arab lovers Qais and Laila (Qais was dubbed Majnun Laila, meaning Laila's madman, because his unrequited love for Laila drove him into madness—and brilliant poetry). What these three star-crossed love stories have in common, though, is that the lovers belonged to hostile/warring groups/tribes and that their love was the cause of a scandal. But then again, "scandal is the lifeblood of love poetry."[39]

It is worth noting that Rita shares many traits that are characteristic of the beloved in Arabic erotic poetry (*ghazal*): she has hazel eyes, marble skin, and long thick tresses; she sings and dances; she is elusive, absent, or otherwise inaccessible; and she belongs to a hostile/warring group. But unlike *ghazal* poetry, where the tension is usually between female desire and patriarchal constraints, in the Rita poems the tension is between the couple's passionate love for each other and political limitations.[40]

Interestingly, the Arabic language has many words for love, each of them denotes a different shade of meaning. The Egyptian woman writer Ahdaf Soueif, in her acclaimed cross-cultural love story, *The Map of Love*, provides the following list:

> "Hubb" is love, "'ishq" is love that entwines two people together, "shaghaf" is love that nests in the chambers of the heart, "hayam" is love that wanders the earth, "teeh" is love in which you lose yourself, "walah" is love that carries sorrow within it, "sababah" is love that exudes from your pores, "hawa" is love that shares its name with "air" and with "falling," "gharam" is love that is willing to pay the price.[41]

Anna Winterbourne, the British heroine of this novel, is destined to experience all these forms of love, including the ultimate love that "is willing to pay the price," when she goes to Egypt and falls for an Egyptian nationalist leader who is assassinated shortly after their marriage. A sweeping narrative that unfolds in three countries—England, Egypt, and the United States—over the course of a century, *The Map of Love* shows how love can blossom between people from different cultures and places and how politics all too often destroys it.

80   D. COHEN-MOR

The Rita poems and prose passages suggest that Darwish had experienced all these forms of love except the last one, "gharam," which is "love that is willing to pay the price." As his poem "The Sleeping Garden" reveals, he had made the agonizing decision to part from Rita even though he loved her: "I love you Rita. I love you. Sleep while I leave." In the final analysis, then, he was no more willing to "pay the price" than Rita was. It would seem that ultimately for Darwish, his patriotic obligations came before love, or his love for his homeland came before his love for Rita, much as for Rita her commitment to her country and to her people came before her love for Darwish. Both, then, have chosen politics over matters of the heart.

NOTES

1. Catherine Belsey, "The Name of the Rose in Romeo and Juliet," in *Romeo and Juliet: William Shakespeare*, ed. R. S. White (New York: Palgrave, 2005), pp. 54–56.
2. The iconic love poem "Rita wa-al-bunduqiyya" was translated into English under the title "Rita and the Gun" by the Jordanian scholar Fawwaz Tuqan and the New Zealand poet Ian Wedde and published in the anthology *Selected Poems: Mahmoud Darwish* (Cheadle Hulme, UK: Carcanet Press, 1973), p. 51. Copyright © 1973 by Ian Wedde. Revised by Ian Wedde. Reprinted (after the Preface in this work) by permission of Ian Wedde. All citations are from this source. For the Arabic text, see Darwish's volume *Akhir al-layl* (Acre: Matba'at al-Jalil, 1967), pp. 44–46; or his collected works, *Al-Diwan: al-a'mal al-ula* (3 vols. Beirut: Riad El-Rayyes, 2005), 1: 200–202.
3. This similarity is pointed out by Kamal Abdel-Malek in *The Rhetoric of Violence: Arab-Jewish Encounters in Contemporary Palestinian Literature and Film* (New York: Palgrave Macmillan, 2005), p. 71.
4. "Birds Die in Galilee" ("Al-'Asafir tamut fi al-Jalil") appears in Darwish, *Al-Diwan: al-a'mal al-ula*, 1: 271–273; translated by Denys Johnson-Davies in *The Music of Human Flesh: Mahmoud Darwish* (Washington, DC: Three Continents Press, 1980), pp. 29–30.
5. Ibid., p. 29.
6. Ibid.
7. Many of Darwish's early poems were first recited at village festivals or first published in magazines and newspapers (such as *al-Jadid* and *al-Ittihad*) and later collected in a volume, where they sometimes underwent slight changes. "Rita, Love Me!" is included in the volume *Birds Die in Galilee* (1969). The phrase "A Song Not Written by Mikis Theodorakis" can be seen in an early translation of this poem by Wedde and Tuqan in *Selected*

Poems: Mahmoud Darwish, pp. 79–82. For the Arabic text, see "Rita …
Ahbini," in Darwish, Al-Diwan: al-aʿmal al-ula, 1: 285–291.

8. All citations are from Wedde and Tuqan's translation of this poem in *Selected Poems: Mahmoud Darwish*, pp. 79–82.

9. Ibid., pp. 79, 80, 81, 82.

10. Ibid., p. 80.

11. "The Sleeping Garden" ("Al-Hadiqa al-naʾima") appears in Darwish, *Al-Diwan: al-aʿmal al-ula*, 2: 309–313; translated by Abdel-Malek in *The Rhetoric of Violence*, pp. 159–161. Cited from p. 160.

12. Ibid.

13. Ibid., p. 161.

14. Ibid., p. 160.

15. Mahmoud Darwish, *Journal of an Ordinary Grief*, trans. Ibrahim Muhawi (Brooklyn: Archipelago Books, 2010). All citations are from this source. For the Arabic text, see *Yawmiyat al-huzn al-ʿadi* in Darwish, *Al-Aʿmal al-jadida al-kamila* (3 vols. Beirut: Riad El-Rayyes, 2009), 3: 351–502.

16. Mahmoud Darwish, *Memory for Forgetfulness: August, Beirut, 1982*, trans. Ibrahim Muhawi (Berkeley: University of California Press, 1995). All citations are from this source. For the Arabic text, see *Dhakira lil-nisyan* in Darwish, *Al-Aʿmal al-jadida al-kamila*, 3: 9–193.

17. "Rita's Winter" ("Shita' Rita") first appeared in Darwish's collection *Eleven Planets*, 1992; reprinted in Darwish, *Al-Diwan: al-aʿmal al-ula*, 3: 331–342; translated by Fady Joudah in *Mahmoud Darwish: If I Were Another* (New York: Farrar, Straus, and Giroux, 2009), pp. 88–93. Cited from p. 93.

18. Until the end of 1966, Arab citizens of Israel lived under martial law, and Darwish needed to obtain a permit to travel from Haifa to Jerusalem, which he was often denied.

19. See Muhawi's explanatory footnote to this line in his translation of Darwish, *Memory for Forgetfulness*, p. 122.

20. Robyn Creswell, "Unbeliever in the Impossible: The Poetry of Mahmoud Darwish." *Harper's Magazine* (February 2009): 69–74. http://search. proquest.com. Accessed 21 December 2016. Cited from the online version, p. 6.

21. "Rita's Winter," trans. Joudah, in *Darwish: If I Were Another*, p. 89.

22. Ibid., p. 93. The elliptical dots are in the original.

23. Ibid., p. 93.

24. Ibid., p. 90.

25. Ibid., p. 89.

26. Ibid., p. 91.

27. Ibid., p. 93.

28. This explanation is based on Jefferson A. Singer and Peter Salovey, *The Remembered Self: Emotion and Memory in Personality* (New York: The Free Press, 1993), p. 41.

29. Ben-Ami's account is presented in Mara'ana-Menuhin's documentary film *Write Down, I Am an Arab* (2014).
30. All these verse citations are from the various translations mentioned previously.
31. Thomas Wheatland, "Sleep and Dreams in Literature." International Institute for Dream Research. www.dreamresearch.ca. Accessed 27 July 2017.
32. Mahmoud Darwish, *Absent Presence* (*Fi hadrat al-ghiyab*, 2006), trans. Mohammad Shaheen (London: Hesperus Press, 2010). All citations are from this source.
33. Subhi Hadidi, "Mahmoud Darwish's Love Poem: History, Exile, and the Epic Call," in *Mahmoud Darwish, Exile's Poet: Critical Essays*, ed. Hala Khamis Nassar and Najat Rahman (Northampton: Olive Branch Press, 2008), pp. 103–105.
34. Ibid., pp. 103–104.
35. "Rita, Love Me!" trans. Wedde and Tuqan, in *Selected Poems: Mahmoud Darwish*, p. 80.
36. "Rita's Winter," trans. Judah, in *Darwish: If I Were Another*, p. 90.
37. Darwish, *Journal of an Ordinary Grief*, p. 52.
38. Darwish, *Absent Presence*, p. 91.
39. Creswell, "Unbeliever in the Impossible," p. 6.
40. Angelika Neuwirth, "Hebrew Bible and Arabic Poetry: Mahmoud Darwish's Palestine—From Paradise Lost to a Homeland Made of Words," in *Mahmoud Darwish, Exile's Poet: Critical Essays*, ed. Khamis and Rahman, pp. 184–185.
41. Ahdaf Soueif, *The Map of Love* (New York: Anchor Books, 1999), pp. 386–387.

CHAPTER 5

Unbeliever in the Impossible

Abstract This chapter examines the implications of the most celebrated love story between a Palestinian man and an Israeli-Jewish woman in recent history. What does it reveal about Darwish's self-definition and his attitude toward the Israeli other? I argue that although Darwish came to be known as a poet of resistance, he had always advocated dialogue with Israelis and embraced the Israeli component in his Palestinian identity. The personal story of these star-crossed lovers illustrates the tragedy of two neighboring communities that have the potential to develop close and enriching ties but are instead embroiled in a century-long conflict. Darwish's resonant words, "We are both unbelievers in the impossible," offer a message of hope for a future resolution of this conflict.

Keywords Mahmoud Darwish—self-definition · Mahmoud Darwish—attitude toward the Israeli other · Mahmoud Darwish and Rita—star-crossed lovers—metaphor for Arab-Jewish relations

The book of Genesis recounts that a famine in the land of Canaan forced Jacob to immigrate with his entire household to Egypt, where his son Joseph, who was appointed the viceroy over the land by Pharaoh, could provide them with food. Jacob lived in Egypt for seventeen years, and when he felt that his end was drawing near, he sent for Joseph and asked him to

© The Author(s) 2019
D. Cohen-Mor, *Mahmoud Darwish*,
https://doi.org/10.1007/978-3-030-24162-9_5

83

84   D. COHEN-MOR

promise that he would bring him to the land of Canaan for burial in the Cave of Machpelah in Hebron, where Abraham and his wife Sarah, as well as Isaac and his wife Rebekah, were buried, and where he had buried his wife Leah. Joseph replied: "'I will do as you have spoken.' And he said, 'Swear to me.' And he swore to him" (Genesis 47:28–31).[1] After Jacob died, Joseph took the necessary steps to carry out his father's last wish. He embalmed Jacob's body in preparation for the long journey, and when the customary period of mourning, as fixed by tradition in Egypt, was over, he requested Pharaoh's permission to leave for Canaan. The rabbinic commentary on this text clarifies that Joseph, being the viceroy of the land, could not leave the country for an extended period without his absence disrupting the work of the government. Therefore, it was necessary for him to secure Pharaoh's permission to leave and also to promise that he would return without delay.[2]

Joseph approached Pharaoh and said, "My father made me swear, saying, 'I am about to die. Be sure to bury me in the grave which I made ready for myself in the land of Canaan.' Now, therefore, let me go up and bury my father; then I shall return." And Pharaoh said, 'Go up and bury your father, as he made you promise on oath'" (Genesis 50:5–6).[3] The medieval Jewish scholar and commentator Rashi (1040–1105) elaborates on the significance of the word *oath* in this exchange, noting that had it not been for the oath, Pharaoh would not have let Joseph leave Egypt. Pharaoh was afraid to tell Joseph to break this oath, lest Joseph would then break the oath he had made to Pharaoh that he would not reveal that he could speak one more language than him. While Pharaoh could converse in seventy languages, Joseph could converse in seventy-one. The additional language that Joseph could speak and Pharaoh could not was the holy tongue—Hebrew. Revelation of this shortcoming would have caused Pharaoh a great embarrassment.[4]

A fascinating *midrash* sheds light on how the oath that Joseph had made to Pharaoh came about. It recounts that when Pharaoh wanted to appoint Joseph the viceroy over Egypt, his advisors were not easily convinced of Joseph's suitability for the task. "You would appoint a slave whose master bought him for twenty pieces of silver over us?" they asked. Pharaoh replied that he had seen marks of nobility in Joseph, whereupon his advisors suggested a test. "If so, he should know seventy languages." Mastery of languages was considered one of the marks of nobility. Joseph received divine help through the agency of the angel Gabriel and was able to converse with Pharaoh in whatever language he spoke to him. But when Joseph spoke to Pharaoh in Hebrew, which was not one of the seventy languages of the nations, he didn't understand what he said. So Pharaoh asked Joseph to teach it to him. Joseph tried, but Pharaoh could not learn it, whereupon he demanded that Joseph should swear not to reveal his embarrassment at not being able to learn Hebrew. Later, when Jacob died and Joseph said to Pharaoh, "My father made me swear to bring him to the land of Canaan for burial," Pharaoh's initial response was, "Go ask to be released from your oath." But Joseph replied, "Then I will also ask to be released from my oath to you." Therefore, although it was displeasing to Pharaoh, he said, "Go up and bury your father, according to what he made you swear."[5]

The curious question that arises is: Why couldn't Pharaoh learn Hebrew? After all, he was an accomplished multilingual and Hebrew is not such a difficult language. The most plausible explanation is that Pharaoh lacked affinity for the people who spoke that language—the Hebrews. The important role of the affective factor in foreign language acquisition is widely acknowledged in the field of linguistics. That the Hebrews, represented by Jacob's children, were held in contempt by the Egyptians is evident from Genesis 43:32–33, which recounts that when Joseph hosted a meal for his brothers and ordered his servants to serve it, "They served him by himself, and them by themselves, and the Egyptians who ate with him by themselves; for the Egyptians could not dine with the Hebrews, since that would be abhorrent to the Egyptians."[6] As the rabbinic commentary elucidates, Joseph ate by himself because of his high status; the Hebrews were segregated because the Egyptians, believing themselves to be racially and religiously superior to all other people, were contemptuous of foreigners.[7] Such a negative attitude toward the "other" supports the assumption that the reason Pharaoh could not learn Hebrew was that he had no empathy for the Hebrews—a group of shepherds from a foreign land who believed in one God. Like his people the Egyptians, Pharaoh worshipped idols and looked down on the activity of shepherding. Learning the language of the Hebrews entailed recognizing their culture, their values, and their creed. Since Pharaoh could not relate to the Hebrews, he could not learn their language.

Mahmoud Darwish, by contrast, could learn Hebrew and spoke it fluently. Shoshana Ditzman Lapidot, the Israeli-Jewish teacher assigned to his high school in Kafr Yasif, taught him the Hebrew language, Hebrew literature, and the Bible. By Darwish's own account, he was influenced by the poetry of Hayim Nahman Bialik, Israel's national poet (1873–1934), especially his poems of longing for the land. "Both of us," he said, "long for the same place. It's only natural that we will speak about winter, a window, the smell of the soil after the first rain. This is the language in which all those who are homesick meet each other."[8] He also appreciated Israel's greatest modern poet Yehuda Amichai (1924–2000), admitting that "his poetry put a challenge to me, because we write about the same place. He wants to use the landscape and history for his own benefit, based on my destroyed identity. So we have a competition: who is the owner of the language of this land? Who loves it more? Who writes it better?"[9] However, Darwish insisted that his rivalry with Amichai was free of animosity: "Poetry and beauty are always making peace. When you read something beautiful you find coexistence; it breaks walls down ... I always humanize the other. ... I will continue to humanize even the enemy."[10] In *al-Karmel*, the literary journal that he edited, he introduced Arab readers to the work of Israeli writers—a rare gesture in the Arab world. As for Shoshana Ditzman Lapidot, his Hebrew teacher, he had only words of praise for her: "She wasn't just a teacher, she was like a mother. It was she who saved me from the fire of hatred. She was a symbol of the good work a Jew does for his people. She taught me how to understand the Bible as a literary work and how to read Bialik for his poetic energy rather than his political message. She never tried to force on us the official curriculum, which sought to alienate us from our cultural heritage. Shoshana saved me from the feelings of resentment with which the military governor had filled me and demolished the walls erected by him."[11] His warm tribute to his Israeli-Jewish teacher shows that his attitude toward Israeli-Jews was not stereotypical.

When asked by Helit Yeshurun in the landmark 1996 interview, "What is Hebrew for you?" Darwish replied, "Hebrew is the first foreign language I learned, at the age of ten or twelve. I spoke in this language with the stranger, the police officer, the military governor, the teacher, the prison guard, and the lover. So it doesn't signify the language of the conqueror, because I spoke words of love in it. It is also the language of my friends. My relationship to it is pure. It opened the door for me to European literature. I read Lorca in Hebrew, as well as Nazim Hikmet, who was required reading in the leftist camp. I first read Greek tragedy in Hebrew. It is also the language of memory for my childhood. When I read Hebrew I am reminded of the place. It brings the landscape with it. Many of my friends in Europe are jealous that I can read the Bible in the original. I haven't stopped reading Hebrew, even Israeli newspapers. And I am interested in the literature, particularly in the poetry. I hope that I will be able to recreate the language. I don't have any complex about it."[12]

Besides acknowledging the pivotal role that Hebrew had played in his education, Darwish also acknowledged that the Israeli other had become a component of his identity: "It is impossible for me to evade the place that the Israeli has occupied in my identity. He exists, whatever I may think of him. He is a physical and psychological fact. The Israelis changed the Palestinians and vice versa. The Israelis are not the same people that came, and the Palestinians are not the same people that once were. In the one, there is the other."[13] He was comfortable with this fact, stressing that his Palestinian identity consists of multiple, heterogeneous elements: "I need heterogeneity. It enriches me."[14] Furthermore, he argued that he can only be defined through the dialectical relationship between himself and the "other." He regarded the Israeli other (Heb. *aher*) as a responsibility (Heb. *ahrayut*) and a test, suggesting that "together we are doing something new in history. ... Will a third way emerge from these two? That is the test."[15]

Not only could Darwish relate to the Hebrew language and to the Israeli other, he was also sensitive to what Israeli poets and writers thought of him. He aspired to be judged by them on the basis of the aesthetic quality of his poetry and not his political views or activities. When his controversial poem "Those Who Are Passing between Fleeting Words" ("'Abirun fi kalam 'abir") was published in 1988, following the outbreak of the first Intifada, it caused an uproar in Israeli society. In this poem he called on the Israelis: "Get out of our native land / Out of our seashore, out of our sea / Out of our wheat, out of our salt, out of our wound / Out of everything, and get out / Of the memories of memory / O you who are passing between passing words."[16] Many Israeli intellectuals interpreted it as a call for the destruction of the State of Israel. Darwish was heavily criticized and condemned in the Israeli media, and even his left-wing friends attacked him, saying that he had crossed the line between revolutionary poetry and war-mongering. In an effort to calm the storm, he wrote a letter to the poet Samih al-Qasim, asserting that his poem was misinterpreted and that he was calling on the Israelis to leave the occupied territories (i.e., the West Bank, Gaza, and East Jerusalem, captured in the Six-Day War in 1967), not the whole country.[17] He did not want his entire poetic work to be judged on the basis of this one poem. "I said what any human being living under occupation would say: Get out of my land," he stated in an interview. "The poem was an expression of protest and anger. I don't consider it a good poem, and I have never included it in my collections for that reason."[18] Deeming the poem too angry and direct, he chose to leave it out of his collected works (*diwan*) as well.

Just as Darwish was denounced by many Israelis for writing "Those Who Are Passing between Fleeting Words," he was denounced by many Arabs for writing the poem "A Soldier Dreams of White Lilies." The subject of this poem is an Israeli soldier who says he wants to stop fighting and live in peace for the sake of his little son. "I refuse to die / turning my gun my love / on women and children / to guard the orchards and wells / of oil tycoons and tycoons of weapons factories."[19] The Israeli soldier, whom the author was supposed to see as a war machine, was seen as flesh and blood. Humanizing the enemy went against the Arabs' stereotypical view of Israelis and was regarded by many as a betrayal. By Darwish's own account, the poem was based on a true encounter with an Israeli soldier who decided to leave the country after returning from the 1967 war. They sat together one night and the soldier told him the story of his life.[20] While the poem minimizes the connection of Israelis to the land, it does give the Israeli a voice and portrays him as a human being rather than as a monster. Besides Darwish, his contemporaries Fadwa Tuqan, in her poem "To Etan," and Fawaz Turki, in his poem "In Search of Yacove Eved,"[21] have also attempted to humanize the enemy amid the rhetoric of violence.

In March 2000, Darwish was embroiled in yet another controversy when the then Israeli minister of education and culture, Yossi Sarid, proposed introducing a few of his poems into the required literature curriculum of high schools. His proposal was heavily criticized by the political right-wing Likud faction in the Knesset and angered the members of the Committee for Literature Instruction, which included academics. The then prime minister Ehud Barak survived a vote of no-confidence, declaring that Israel was "not ready" for this kind of poetry. In an interview for the *New York Times*, Darwish expressed his disappointment at this outcome: "The Israelis don't want to teach students that there is a love story between an Arab poet and this land. ... I just wish they'd read me to enjoy my poetry, not as a representative of the enemy."[22]

In July 2016, Darwish, already deceased, was again at the center of a political storm when the IDF radio channel Galei Tzahal broadcast a program about him in which the poem "Identity Card" was recited and discussed. Miri Regev, then the minister of education, and Avigdor Liberman, then the minister of defense, attacked the program and denounced the commander of Galei Tzahal for allowing an inflammatory poem that opposes the very existence of Israel as a democratic Jewish state to be broadcast to the public. Leading Israeli poets, writers, and intellectuals weighed in on the issue. The poet Haim Guri asked, "What is the wisdom in not reading Mahmoud Darwish? He is the national poet of the people who are fighting with us. If we want this fight to end one day, and not in death, we have to get to know him."[23] The poet Eliaz Cohen said, "I too find it hard to relate to some of Darwish's poems, but they are part of the Israeli-Palestinian conflict. How are we to deal with this conflict if we don't know them? Poetry represents the innermost feelings and thoughts of a people's culture and society."[24] Although Darwish's standing in Israeli society continues to be tied to the political climate, he has by now become the most translated Palestinian poet into Hebrew: several volumes of his poetry have been translated in their entirety into Hebrew, and leading literary magazines, as well as newspaper literary supplements, publish translations of his poems.[25]

Despite his critical stance toward the Oslo Accords, Darwish had always advocated dialogue with Israelis. "I don't have a pure Arab cultural identity," he asserted. "I'm the result of a mixture of civilizations in Palestine's past. I don't monopolize history and memory and God, as Israelis want to do. They put the past on the battlefield. ... We shouldn't fight about the past. Let each one tell his narrative as he wants. Let the two narratives make a dialogue, and history will smile."[26] The poet Zakaria Mohammed characterizes all of Darwish's poetry as "a conversation between him and the Israelis to find a spot where they can reconcile."[27] Darwish repeatedly said that "the first teacher who taught me Hebrew was a Jew. The first love affair in my life was with a Jewish girl. The first judge who sent me to prison was a Jewish woman. So from the beginning, I didn't see Jews as devils or angels but as human beings."[28] Witness all the poems to Rita, his Jewish lover, poems that take the side of love, not war.

The Rita poems and prose passages reveal a chapter in Darwish's life that left a lasting emotional mark on him. This unforgettable event in his life—his first experience of romantic love, and an unrequited love at that—became seared in his mind as a self-defining memory with a close linkage to his national identity and the loss of his homeland. Unhappy self-defining memories, say the psychologists Jefferson A. Singer and Peter Salovey, are organized around an important unresolved issue or enduring concern in one's life. Individuals may repetitively recall unpleasant self-defining memories because they are still struggling to work through and resolve the issue expressed by them: "Only by reviving the memories into consciousness do individuals avail themselves of an opportunity to recast the meaning of previous events or to re-imagine them in a way that is more palatable to their self-image."[29] That is why Rita is evoked again and again in Darwish's poems, like a haunting dream or an obsession. As a dominant leitmotif with an adaptive function, the Rita memories have undoubtedly played a role in Darwish's process of self-understanding and in his creative evolution as a poet.

What is the larger significance of this particular chapter in Darwish's life, a chapter that, as he writes in his iconic poem "Rita and the Gun," lasted two whole years? The answer, as often, can be found in one of his many other poems. It is pertinent to note that Darwish had unconventional ideas about his biography and, dismissing the need to write it, argued that "what matters to the reader about my biography is in my poems. There is a saying that every musical poem is an autobiography."[30] Seen in this light, a particular line in Darwish's love poem "A Beautiful Woman in Sodom" seems to hold the answer to the question posed above. In this poem, the poet-speaker says to his beloved, "We are both unbelievers in the impossible" (*wa-kilana kafirun bi-al-mustahil*).[31] The literary critic Robyn Creswell has pointed out that this is an ambiguous line that lends itself to contrasting interpretations. On the one hand, it might mean believing that anything is possible, even a happy ending to a love story across ethno-religious lines. On the other hand, it might mean that we do not believe in the impossible because we know better than to put our faith in it.[32] Both senses are present in Darwish's love poems. Which one wins out? Was Darwish an optimist or a pessimist? The answer to this question lies, again, in one of his other poems, "On This Earth," which appears in what is regarded as his best volume, *Fewer Roses* (1986). In this poem, Darwish repeats the line "We have on this earth what makes life worth living" three times, like a refrain, each time enumerating other compelling reasons or worthwhile experiences, central among them are "the beginning of love" and "the Lady of Earth," that is, Palestine.[33] This poem may well have been his credo. It reveals that despite his many trials and tribulations, he retained a positive outlook on life and a sense of optimism. Fittingly, this line was selected to be engraved on his tombstone in Ramallah, where he was laid to rest.

The personal story of the star-crossed lovers recounted in the Rita poems and prose passages is ultimately a metaphor for Arab-Jewish relations. It is customary in literature worldwide to depict a conflict between two ethno-religious groups by describing a relationship between a man and a woman. "This serves as a model, for success or failure, of a developing pattern of relations between two antagonistic sides—in this case [i.e., Arabs and Jews] between two nations," says the Israeli scholar Nurit Govrin. "These portrayals are part of the more comprehensive treatment of attraction and rejection, or erotic nightmare and desire. The stranger, the savage, the primitive, the black—these, in all cultures, have a powerful fascination, frightening and thrilling at one and the same time."[34] Hence the wealth of stories and novels in Hebrew literature depicting the attraction between the sexes from opposite sides of the divide, usually a Jewish woman and an Arab man, and occasionally a Jewish man and an Arab woman. Although in most of these works of fiction such relationships end in failure, a heightened sense of awareness of the common humanity and intertwined destinies of the two adversarial sides emerges from the narratives. The Rita poems and prose passages illustrate the tragedy of two neighboring communities that have the potential to develop close and enriching ties but instead are embroiled in a century-long conflict. Darwish's resonant words, "We are both unbelievers in the impossible," offer a message of hope that this seemingly unresolvable conflict will someday come to an end.

NOTES

1. *JPS Hebrew-English Tanakh* (Philadelphia: The Jewish Publication Society, 1999), p. 104.
2. *The Chumash*, ed. rabbi Nosson Scherman and rabbi Meir Zlotowitz (Brooklyn: Menorah Publications, 1966), Genesis 50:4–6, p. 285.
3. *JPS Hebrew-English Tanakh*, p. 110.
4. *The Chumash*, Genesis 50:6, p. 284.
5. *Babylonian Talmud*: Sotah 36b. See also Avner Zarmi, "This Week's Torah Portion: Why Couldn't the Pharaoh Learn Hebrew?" (29 December 2016). http://pjmedia.com. Accessed 1 December 2017.
6. *JPS Hebrew-English Tanakh*, p. 94.
7. *Etz Hayim: Torah and Commentary*, ed. David L. Lieber et al. (Philadelphia: Jewish Publications Society, 2001), Genesis 43:32–33, p. 267.
8. Mahmoud Darwish, "Hagalut kol kach hazaka betochi," a landmark interview conducted by Helit Yeshurun, *Hadarim: Magazine for Poetry* 12 (Spring 1996): 198. Translation mine. This segment is not included in the abridged English version, "Exile Is So Strong Within Me, I May Bring It to the Land," trans. Adam Yale Stern, published in *Journal of Palestine Studies* 42, no. 1 (Autumn 2012): 46–70.
9. Maya Jaggi, "Poet of the Arab World: Mahmoud Darwish." *The Guardian* (7 June 2002), pp. 3–4. http://www.theguardian.com/books. Accessed 12 August 2016.
10. Ibid.

92   D. COHEN-MOR

11. *Al-Jadid* (December 1969), p. 28. Cited in Reuven Snir, *Mahmoud Darwish: hamishim shnot shira* (Tel Aviv: Keshev, 2015), p. 46. Translation mine.

12. Darwish, "Exile Is So Strong Within Me," p. 69.

13. Ibid., pp. 68–69.

14. Ibid., p. 69.

15. Ibid., pp. 68 and 69 respectively.

16. This poem is translated by Kamal Abdel-Malek in *The Rhetoric of Violence: Arab-Jewish Encounters in Contemporary Palestinian Literature and Film* (New York: Palgrave Macmillan, 2005), pp. 154–155. This citation is reproduced with permission of Springer Nature Service Center.

17. Muna Abu Eid, *Mahmoud Darwish: Literature and the Politics of Palestinian Identity* (London: I. B. Tauris, 2016), pp. 140–142.

18. Cited from "A Love Story between an Arab Poet and His Land," an interview with Mahmoud Darwish by Adam Shatz, *Journal of Palestine Studies* 31, no. 3 (Spring 2002), p. 71. See also Adam Shatz, "A Poet's Palestine as a Metaphor." *The New York Times* (22 December 2001), p. 3. http://www.nytimes.com. Accessed 16 August 2016; and Jaggi, "Poet of the Arab World," p. 6.

19. "A Soldier Dreams of White Lilies" ("Jundi yahlam bi-al-zanabiq al-bayda'") first appeared in Darwish's collection *The End of the Night*, 1968; reprinted in Darwish, *Al-Diwan: al-a'mal al-ula* (Beirut: Riad El-Rayyes, 2005), 1: 203–209; translated by Ian Wedde and Fawwaz Tuqan in *Selected Poems: Mahmoud Darwish* (Cheadle Hulme, UK: Carcanet, 1973), pp. 56–58. Cited from p. 58.

20. Darwish, "Exile Is So Strong Within Me," pp. 59–60. See also Snir, *Mahmoud Darwish: hamishim shnot shira*, p. 79.

21. Fadwa Tuqan, "To Etan" appears in *Women of the Fertile Crescent: Modern Poetry by Arab Women*, ed. Kamal Boullata (Colorado Springs: Three Continents Press, 1981), p. 156; Fawaz Turki, "In Search of Yacove Eved" appears in *Anthology of Modern Palestinian Literature*, ed. Salma Khadra Jayyusi (New York: Columbia University Press, 1992), p. 366.

22. Cited from "A Love Story between an Arab Poet and His Land," an interview with Mahmoud Darwish, p. 71.

23. Cited in Gili Izikovich, "Mahmoud Darwish: 'Fuel for Terrorism' or a Poet That Israelis Must Get to Know?" (in Hebrew). *Haaretz* (20 July 2016), p. 3. https://www.haaretz.co.il. Accessed 12 August 2016. Translation mine.

24. Ibid. Translation mine.

25. For example, the Israeli scholar Reuven Snir has published the book *Mahmoud Darwish: hamishim shnot shira* (Fifty Years of Poetry) (Tel Aviv:

Keshev, 2015), which contains an extensive introduction to Darwish's life and work as well as many translations from his poetry.

26. Jaggi, "Poet of the Arab World," p. 7.

27. Ibid., p. 7.

28. Ibid., p. 4.

29. Jefferson A. Singer and Peter Salovey, *The Remembered Self: Emotion and Memory in Personality* (New York: The Free Press, 1993), pp. 40–41.

30. Cited from the website of Mahmoud Darwish Foundation, under "biography," p. 1. http://www.darwishfoundation.org. Accessed 14 August 2016.

31. "A Beautiful Woman in Sodom" ("Imra'a jamila fi Sudum") first appeared in Darwish's collection *Birds Die in Galilee*, 1969; reprinted in Darwish, *Al-Diwan: al-a'mal al-ula*, 1: 305–309. Cited from p. 306.

32. Robyn Creswell, "Unbeliever in the Impossible: The Poetry of Mahmoud Darwish," *Harper's Magazine* (February 2009), pp. 69–74. http://search.proquest.com. Accessed 21 December 2016. Cited from the online version, p. 6.

33. For a translation of "On This Earth," see *Mahmoud Darwish: Unfortunately, It Was Paradise: Selected Poems*, trans. Munir Akash and Carolyn Force (with Sinan Antoon and Amira El-Zein) (Berkeley: University of California Press, 2003), p. 6. Cited from this source. For the Arabic text, see "'Ala hadhihi al-ard" in Darwish, *Al-Diwan: al-a'mal al-ula*, 3: 111–112.

34. Nurit Govrin, "Enemies or Cousins? … Somewhere in Between. The Arab Problem and Its Reflection in Hebrew Literature: Developments, Trends, and Examples," *Shofar* 7, no. 3 (Spring 1989): 19.

BIBLIOGRAPHY

Abd al-Quddus, Ihsan. *Far from Land*. In his collection *I Am Free and Other Stories*, translated by Trevor Le Gassick, pp. 227–249. Cairo: General Egyptian Book Organization, 1978.

Abdel-Malek, Kamal. *The Rhetoric of Violence: Arab-Jewish Encounters in Contemporary Palestinian Literature and Film*. New York: Palgrave Macmillan, 2005.

———. *Come with Me from Jerusalem*. United Arab Emirates, 2013.

Abduh, Wazin. *Mahmud Darwish, al-gharib yaqaʿu ʿala nafsihi: qiraʾa fi aʿmalihi al-jadida*. Beirut: Dar al-Zahra, 2006.

Abudi, Dalya. *Mothers and Daughters in Arab Women's Literature: The Family Frontier*. Leiden: Brill, 2011.

Abu Eid, Muna. *Mahmoud Darwish: Literature and the Politics of Palestinian Identity*. London: I. B. Tauris, 2016.

Abu Ghush, Usama. *Ke-Yehudi bein yehudim: sipur ahava* (As a Jew Among Jews: A Love Story). Raanana: The Institute for Israeli-Arab Studies, 1995.

Abu Murad, Fathi Muhammad. *Al-Ramz al-fanni fi shiʿr Mahmud Darwish*. Amman, 2004.

Adnan, Etel. *Sitt Marie Rose*. Sausalito: Post-Apollo Press, 1982.

Amir, Eli. *Yasmin*. (Hebrew, 2005). Translated by Yael Lotan. London: Halban, 2012.

Assadi, Mysoon. "Forbidden Talk." In *Loud Sounds from the Holy Land: Short Fiction by Palestinian Women*, edited and translated by Jamal Assadi with assistance from Martha Moody, pp. 57–60. New York: Peter Lang, 2011.

Al Aswany, Alaa. *Chicago*. Translated by Farouk Abdel Wahab. Cairo: American University in Cairo Press, 2007.

96 BIBLIOGRAPHY

Athamneh, Waed. *Modern Arabic Poetry: Revolution and Conflict.* Notre Dame: University of Notre Dame Press, 2017.

Atlas, Yehuda. "Shelakh, Mahmoud" (Yours, Mahmoud). *Yediot Ahronot,* 7 days (25 March 1988), pp. 42–44.

Ballas, Shimon. *Heder na'ul* (A Locked Room). Tel Aviv: Zmora, Bitan, Modan, 1980.

Bamia, Aida A. "The Image of the Jew in Arabic Literature: The Case of Some Palestinian Writers." *Shofar* 7, no. 3 (Spring 1989): 32–42.

Baydas, Khalil. *Al-Warith* (The Heir, 1920). Ramallah: Alraqamia, 2011.

Belsey, Catherine. "The Name of the Rose in Romeo and Juliet." In *Romeo and Juliet: William Shakespeare,* edited by R. S. White, pp. 47–67. New York: Palgrave, 2001.

Ben-Ezer, Ehud, ed. *Sleepwalkers and Other Stories: The Arab in Hebrew Fiction.* Boulder: Lynne Rienner, 1999.

Boullata, Issa J. "Mahmoud Darwish: Identity and Change." In *Israeli and Palestinian Identities in History and Literature,* edited by Kamal Abdel-Malek and David J. Jacobson, pp. 159–166. New York: St. Martin's Press, 1999.

Brenner, Rachel Feldhay. *Inextricably Bonded: Israeli Arab and Jewish Writers Revisioning Culture.* Madison: University of Wisconsin Press, 2003.

Bulos, Nassib D. *Jerusalem Crossroads.* Beirut: Dar al-Nahar, 2003.

Cohen-Mor, Dalya. *A Matter of Fate: The Concept of Fate in the Arab World as Reflected in Modern Arabic Literature.* New York: Oxford University Press, 2001.

———. *Fathers and Sons in the Arab Middle East.* New York: Palgrave Macmillan, 2013.

———, ed. *Arab Women Writers: An Anthology of Short Stories.* Albany: State University of New York Press, 2005.

———, ed. *Cultural Journeys into the Arab World: A Literary Anthology.* Albany: State University of New York Press, 2018.

Cook, Jonathan. "In Israel Intermarriage Viewed as Treason." *The Electronic Intifada* (25 September 2009). https://www.electronicintifada.net. Accessed 28 August 2016.

Creswell, Robyn. "Unbeliever in the Impossible: The Poetry of Mahmoud Darwish." *Harper's Magazine* (February 2009): 69–74. http://search.proquest.com. Accessed 21 December 2016.

Darwish, Mahmoud. *Selected Poems.* Introduced and translated by Ian Wedde and Fawwaz Tuqan. Cheadle Hulme, UK: Carcanet, 1973.

———. *Splinters of Bone: Poems.* Selected and translated by B. M. Bennani. New York: The Greenfield Review Press, 1974.

———. *The Music of Human Flesh.* Selected and translated by Denys-Johnson Davies. Washington, DC: Three Continents Press, 1980.

———. *Sand and Other Poems.* Translated by Rana Qabbani. London: Kegan Paul, 1986.

BIBLIOGRAPHY 97

———. *Psalms*. Translated by Ben Bennani. Colorado Springs: Three Continents Press, 1994.

———. *Memory for Forgetfulness: August, Beirut, 1982*. Translated by Ibrahim Muhawi. Berkeley: University of California Press, 1995.

———. "Hagalut kol kach hazaka betochi." A landmark 1996 interview with Mahmoud Darwish by Helit Yeshurun (in Hebrew). *Hadarim: Magazine for Poetry* 12 (Spring 1996): 172–198.

———. *The Adam of Two Edens: Poems*. Edited by Munir Akash and Daniel Moore. Syracuse: Jusoor and Syracuse University Press, 2000.

———. "A Love Story between an Arab Poet and His Land." An interview with Mahmoud Darwish by Adam Shatz. *Journal of Palestine Studies* 31, no. 3 (Spring 2002): 67–78.

———. *Unfortunately, It Was Paradise: Selected Poems*. Translated and edited by Munir Akash and Carolyn Forche (with Sinan Antoon and Amira El-Zein). Berkeley: University of California Press, 2003.

———. *Al-Diwan: al-a'mal al-ula* (The Early Collected Works). 3 vols. Beirut: Riad El-Rayyes, 2005.

———. *Why Did You Leave the Horse Alone?* Translated by Jeffrey Sacks. Brooklyn: Archipelago Books, 2006.

———. *The Butterfly's Burden: Poems*. Translated by Fady Joudah. Port Townsend: Copper Canyon Press, 2007.

———. *Almond Blossoms and Beyond*. Translated by Mohammad Shaheen. Northampton: Interlink Books, 2009.

———. *I Wish I Were Another: Poems*. Translated by Fady Joudah. New York: Farrar, Straus, and Giroux, 2009.

———. *A River Dies of Thirst: Journals*. Translated by Catherine Cobham. Brooklyn: Archipelago Books, 2009.

———. *Al-A'mal al-jadida al-kamila* (The New Collected Works). 3 vols. Beirut: Riad El-Rayyes, 2009.

———. *Journal of an Ordinary Grief*. Translated by Ibrahim Muhawi. Brooklyn: Archipelago Books, 2010.

———. *Absent Presence*. Translated by Mohammad Shaheen. London: Hesperus Press, 2010.

———. *A State of Siege*. Translated by Munir Akash and Daniel Moore. Syracuse: Jusoor and Syracuse University Press, 2010.

———. "Exile Is So Strong Within Me, I May Bring It to the Land." An abridged version of the landmark 1996 interview with Mahmoud Darwish by Helit Yeshurun. Translated from Hebrew by Adam Yale Stern. *Journal of Palestine Studies* 42, no. 1 (Autumn 2012): 46–70.

———. *I Don't Want This Poem to End: Early and Late Poems*. Edited and translated by Mohammad Shaheen. Northampton: Interlink Books, 2017.

———. Mahmoud Darwish Foundation. http://www.darwishfoundation.org.

98 BIBLIOGRAPHY

Fayyad, Suleiman. *Voices.* Translated by Hosam Aboul-Ela. New York: Marion Boyars, 1993.

Ferber, Alona. "When the Palestinian National Poet Fell in Love with a Jew." *Haaretz* (4 June 2014). https://www.haaretz.com. Accessed 12 August 2017.

Fishere, Ezzedine C. *Embrace on Brooklyn Bridge.* Translated by John Peate. New York: Hoopoe, 2017.

Forbidden Marriages in the Holy Land. Directed by Michel Khleifi. DVD. Seattle: Arab Film Distribution, 1995.

Ghanem, As'ad. *The Palestinian-Arab Minority in Israel, 1948-2000: A Political Study.* Albany: State University of New York Press, 2001.

Goodman, Amy. "Mahmoud Darwish, Poet Laureate of the Palestinians, 1941–2008." *Democracy Now* (11 August 2008). www.democracynow.org. Accessed 14 November 2016.

Govrin, Nurit. "Enemies or Cousins? ... Somewhere in Between. The Arab Problem and Its Reflection in Hebrew Literature: Developments, Trends, and Examples." *Shofar* 7, no. 3 (Spring 1989): 13–23.

Hadidi, Subhi. "Mahmoud Darwish's Love Poem: History, Exile, and the Epic Call." In *Mahmoud Darwish, Exile's Poet: Critical Essays,* edited by Hala Khamis Nassar and Najat Rahman, pp. 95–122. Northampton: Olive Branch Press, 2008.

Hamza, Husayn. *Murawaghat al-nass: dirasat fi shi'r Mahmud Darwish.* Haifa: Maktabat kull shay', 2001.

Hareven, Alouph, ed. *Every Sixth Israeli: Relations between the Jewish Majority and Arab Minority in Israel.* Jerusalem: Van Leer Jerusalem Foundation, 1983.

Idris, Yusuf. *The Sinners.* Translated by Kristin Peterson-Ishaq. Washington, DC: Three Continents Press, 1984.

———. "Egyptian Mona Lisa." In *Yusuf Idris: The Piper Dies and Other Stories,* translated by Dalya Cohen-Mor with Francis Liardet, pp. 1–25. Potomac, MD: Sheba Press, 1992.

al-Iryani, Ramziya Abbas. *Al-Ghariba* (The Stranger). In her collection *Al-Sama' tumtiru qutnan* (The Sky is Raining Cotton). Sana'a, 1999.

Jacobson, David C. "Intimate Relations Between Israelis and Palestinians in Fiction by Israeli Women writers." *Shofar* 25, no. 3 (Spring 2007): 32–46.

Jaggi, Maya. "Poet of the Arab world: Mahmoud Darwish." *The Guardian* (7 June 2002). https://theguardian.com/books. Accessed 12 August 2016.

Jayyusi, Salma Khadra, ed. *Modern Arabic Poetry: An Anthology.* New York: Columbia University Press, 1987.

———, ed. *Anthology of Modern Palestinian Literature.* New York: Columbia University Press, 1992.

Kashua, Sayed. *Dancing Arabs* (*Aravim rokdim,* 2002). Translated by Miriam Shlesinger. New York: Grove Press, 2004.

Le Gassick, Trevor. "The Image of the Jew in Post-World War II Arabic Literature." *Al-Arabiyya* 11, no. 1–2 (Spring and Autumn 1978): 74–89.

———. "The Image of the Jew in Modern Arabic Fiction." *Shofar* 7, no. 3 (Spring 1989): 43–57.

Liebrecht, Savyon. "A Room on the Roof," translated by Jeffrey M. Green. In her collection *Apples from the Desert: Selected Stories*, pp. 39–64. New York: Feminist Press, 1998.

Lopes, Margarida Santos. "Darwish Through the Eyes of Three Women—One of Them His Jewish Lover." http://margaridasantoslopes.com. Accessed 10 September 2017.

Mansour, Atallah. *In a New Light* (*Be'or hadash*, 1966). Translated by Abraham Birman. London: Vallentine, Mitchell, 1969.

Mansson, Anette. *Passage to a New Wor(l)d: Exile and Restoration in Mahmoud Darwish's Writings 1960–1995*. Uppsala: Uppsala Universitet, 2003.

Mar'i, Sami Khalil. *Arab Education in Israel*. Syracuse: Syracuse University Press, 1978.

Mattawa, Khaled. *Mahmoud Darwish: The Poet's Art and His Nation*. Syracuse: Syracuse University Press, 2014.

Mendelson-Maoz, Adia. *Multiculturalism in Israel: Literary Perspectives*. West Lafayette: Purdue University Press, 2014.

Meri, Josef, ed. *The Routledge Handbook of Muslim-Jewish Relations*. London: Routledge, 2016.

Michael, Sami. *A Trumpet in the Wadi* (*Hatsotsra ba-vadi*, 1987). Translated by Yael Lotan. New York: Simon & Schuster, 2003.

al-Naqqash, Raja'. *Mahmud Darwish: sha'ir al-ard al-muhtalla*. Cairo: Dar al-Hilal, 1969.

Nassar, Hala Khamis, and Najat Rahman, eds. *Mahmoud Darwish, Exile's Poet: Critical Essays*. Northampton: Olive Branch Press, 2008.

Nye, Naomi Shihab. *Habibi*. New York: Simon Pulse, 1997.

Oz, Amos. *Nomad and Viper*. In his collection *Where the Jackals Howl and Other Stories*, translated by Nicholas de Lange and Philip Simpson, pp. 21–38. New York: Harcourt Brace Jovanovich, 1981.

Peleg, Michal. "Ha-Yehudiya ha-tova" (The Good Jewess). In her collection *Shir heres ve-sipurim aherim* (Ruin Song and Other Stories), pp. 33–55. Tel Aviv: Ha-Kibbutz Ha-Meuhad, 1996.

Pew Research Center. "Israel's Religiously Divided Society" (8 March 2016). http://www.pewform.org. Accessed 15 June 2017.

100 BIBLIOGRAPHY

Rabinyan, Dorit. *All the Rivers* (*Gader haya*, 2014). Translated by Jessica Cohen. New York: Random House, 2017.

Racin, Limore, and Simon Dein. "Jewish-Arab Couple Relationships in Israel: Underlying Motives for Entering and Engaging in Intermarriage." *Journal of Muslim Mental Health* 5 (2010): 278–300.

Ramras-Rauch, Gila. *The Arab in Israeli Literature*. Bloomington: Indiana University Press, 1989.

Al-Shahham, Abdullah. "A Portrait of the Israeli Woman as the Beloved: The Woman-Soldier in the Poetry of Mahmud Darwish after the 1967 War." *Bulletin* (*British Society for Middle Eastern Studies*) 15, no. 1–2 (1988): 28–49.

Shakour, Adel. "Arab Authors in Israel Writing in Hebrew: Fleeting Fashion or Persistent Phenomenon?" *Language Problems and Language Planning* 37, no. 1 (Spring 2013): 1–17.

Shipler, David K. *Arab and Jew: Wounded Spirits in a Promised Land*. Rev. ed. New York: Broadway Books, 2015.

Sikseck, Ayman. *El Yafo* (To Jaffa). Tel Aviv: Yediot Ahronot and Hemed Books, 2010.

Singer, Jefferson A., and Peter Salovey. *The Remembered Self: Emotion and Memory in Personality*. New York: The Free Press, 1993.

Smooha, Sammy. *Arabs and Jews in Israel*. 2 vols. Boulder: Westview Press, 1989–1992.

Snir, Reuven. *Mahmoud Darwish: hamishim shnot shira* (Fifty Years of Poetry). Tel Aviv: Keshev, 2015.

Soueif, Ahdaf. *The Map of Love*. New York: Anchor Books, 2000.

Sternberg, Robert J., and Karin Weis, eds. *The New psychology of Love*. New Haven: Yale University Press, 2006.

Al-Tahawy, Miral. *Brooklyn Heights* (*Murtafaʻat Bruklin*, 2010). Translated by Sameh Salim. London: Faber and Faber, 2012.

Timmer, Jaap. "Dangerous Liaisons: Perceptions on Arab/Jewish Intermarriage in Israel." *Culture Matters* (9 August 2011). http://culturematters.com. Accessed 20 November 2016.

Wheatland, Thomas. "Sleep and Dreams in Literature." The International Institute for Dream Research. www.dreamreseach.ca. Accessed 27 July 2017.

Write Down, I Am an Arab. Directed, filmed, and produced by Ibtisam Maraʻana-Menuhin. DVD. Tel Aviv: Ibtisam Films, 2014.

Yehoshua, A. B. *The Lover* (*Ha-Meʼahev*, 1977). Translated by Philip Simpson. New York: Doubleday, 1978.

INDEX

A

Abd al-Quddus, Ihsan
   Far from Land, 19–21, 42
Abdel-Malek, Kamal, 12, 23, 55, 80
   Come with Me from Jerusalem, 23, 42
Abu Eid, Muna, 3, 10, 54, 61, 92
Abu Ghush, Usama, 24
   As a Jew Among Jews: A Love Story, 26–27, 28, 42
Adnan, Etel
   Sitt Marie Rose, 14, 41
al-Ahram (newspaper), 7, 54
Akash, Munir, 7, 10, 12, 93
Amichai, Yehuda, 4, 38, 86
Amir, Eli, 34
   Yasmine, 34, 35, 39–40, 43
Arab-Israeli conflict, 19, 34, 39, 76, 91
   the 1948 war (the Nakba), 3, 26, 77
   the first Intifada (1987-1993), 55
   the invasion of Lebanon (1982), 26, 35, 38, 72
   the October 1973 War, 26, 35
   the Six-Day War (June 1967), 26, 39, 51, 53, 55, 87

Arab-Jewish mixed marriages. *See also* romance across ethno-religious lines
   the Bible on interfaith marriage, 15
   children's identity, according to Jewish law, 16
   children's identity, according to Muslim law, 16
   incidence of, in Israel, 14, 15, 16, 35, 47, 48, 49
   the Koran on interfaith marriage, 16
   social attitudes of Arabs toward, 14, 15, 17, 46–47
   social attitudes of Jews toward, 14, 16–17, 38, 46–47
   viewed as treason, 14, 41
Arafat, Yasser, 56
Assadi, Maysoon
   "Forbidden Talk,", 32, 42
Al Aswany, Alaa
   Chicago, 22–23, 42
Atallah, Mansour
   In a New Light, 24, 30–32, 42
Atlas, Yehuda, 47, 49, 61
Awad, Mira, 48, 66

102 INDEX

B

Ballas, Shimon
  A Locked Room, 34
Baydas, Khalil
  Al-Warith, 21, 42
Ben-Ami, Tamar
  birth and childhood, 48
  career as a dancer and choreographer,
    53, 55–56, 59, 67
  education, 48, 50, 51
  last meeting with Darwish, 56–57,
    76
  love letters from Darwish, 46, 47,
    49–50, 51, 52–53, 59
  love story with Darwish, 47, 48–51,
    52–53, 56–57, 59
  member of the Israeli Communist
    Youth Alliance, 48–50
Bialik, Hayim Nahman, 4, 85, 86
Bible
  Joseph's oath to Jacob, 83–84
  midrash on Joseph's oath to
    Pharaoh, 84–85
  why Pharaoh couldn't learn Hebrew,
    85
al-Birwa, 3
Bulos, Nassib D.
  Jerusalem Crossroads, 24–25, 26, 32,
    42

C

Cohen, Eliaz, 89
Creswell, Robyn, 5, 10, 11, 81, 82, 90,
  93

D

Darwish, Mahmoud
  advocated dialogue with Israelis, 89
  attitude toward the Israeli other, 86,
    87, 88, 89
  birth and childhood, 3
  collected works (*diwan*), 55, 68, 87
  concept of his Palestinian identity,
    61, 87, 89

  concept of *watan*, 3
  contribution to Palestinian literature
    and culture, v, 8, 59
  criticism of, by Arabs, 7, 8, 54, 88
  death, 8, 59, 77, 90
  desire for aesthetic control over his
    poetry, 7, 9
  education, 4, 7, 85, 86
  and Hebrew language, 4, 85, 87
  and the Israeli Communist Party
    (Rakah), 4, 7, 48
  journalistic work, 4, 8, 54, 59, 86
  key figure in the PLO, 4, 54
  literary influences on, 4, 48, 85–86
  living in exile, 7, 8, 53–54
  living in Haifa, 4, 48
  living in Ramallah, 8, 59
  "lover from Palestine", 1, 2, 5, 68
  love story with Tamar Ben-Ami, 4,
    48–51, 52–53, 56–57, 59
  lyrical poetry, 2, 8, 59
  meditation on sleep, 77–78
  patriotic poetry, 2, 6
  personal life, 54–55
  personified the homeland as the
    beloved, 5–6
  poet of national resistance, 5, 7, 9,
    54, 58
  prison experiences and house arrests,
    4, 51–52
  public adulation of, 7, 9
  public persona of, 3, 6, 9
  readers' expectations of, 7, 8–9
  relations with left-wing intellectuals
    in Israel, 55, 87–89
  Rita as a leitmotif, 59, 77, 90
  spokesperson for his people, 5
  stages in his poetic career, 5, 53–54
  subject of political controversy in
    Israel, 47, 87, 88
  tensions between his poetic quest
    and public expectations, 5, 7,
    8–9

INDEX 103

translations of his poems into Hebrew, 89, 92n25

view of how a love affair should end, 78–79

view of sex as honeyed death, 74

Darwish, Mahmoud, poems
"A Beautiful Woman in Sodom", 73, 90, 93
"Birds Die in Galilee", 66–68, 73
"A Certain Hymn", 10
"Diary of a Palestinian Wound", 2, 10
"The Eternity of Cactus", 3
"The Hoopoe", 1, 10
"I Am the Unlucky Lover", 6, 10
"Identity Card", 5, 11, 53, 88
"Longing for the Light", 7, 11
"A Lover from Palestine", 2, 6, 10, 11, 53, 68
"The Most Beautiful Love", 5
"Mural", 9
"On This Earth", 90, 93
"Reading My Beloved's Face", 6
"Rita and the Gun", 48, 53, 58, 66, 67, 76, 77, 80, 90
"Rita, Love Me!", 66, 68, 69, 77, 78, 80, 82
"Rita's Winter", 66, 72, 75–78, 81, 82
"The Sleeping Garden", 66, 69, 70, 75, 77, 78, 80
"A Soldier Dreams of White Lilies", 88, 92
"Those Who Are Passing between Fleeting Words", 55, 87, 88
"To My End and to Its End", 3
"To My Mother", 3, 7, 10, 11, 53
"Writing in the Light of a Rifle", 57, 63

Darwish, Mahmoud, prose works
Absent Presence, 77, 78, 82

Journal of an Ordinary Grief, 8, 51, 53, 66, 70, 78, 81
Memory for Forgetfulness, 5, 8, 66, 72–74, 81

F

Fayyad, Suleiman
Voices, 18, 41
Fishere, Ezzedine Choukri
Embrace on Brooklyn Bridge, 18
flashbulb memories, 59

G

Galei Tzahal, 88
Ghanayim, Muhammad Hamza, 55
ghazal poetry, 79
Govrin, Nurit, 90, 93
Guri, Haim, 88

H

Habibi, Emile, 4, 48
Hadidi, Subhi, 8, 9, 78
Haqqi, Yahya
The Saint's Lamp, 18
Heeni, Hayat, 54
Hikmet, Nazim, 50, 86
Hourani, Hassan
and relationship with Dorit Rabinyan, 37, 43n46

I

Idris, Suhayl
The Latin Quarter, 18
Idris, Yusuf, 7, 18, 54
"Egyptian Mona Lisa", 17, 41
The Sinners, 18, 41
al-Iryani, Ramziya Abbas
The Stranger, 19, 42
Israeli Communist Party (Rakah), 4, 7, 35, 48–50, 53, 54

104 INDEX

Israeli Communist Youth Alliance
(Banki), 48, 62n12
al-Ittihad (newspaper), 4, 48, 80

J
al-Jadid (newspaper), 4, 48, 49, 80
al-Jadida, 3, 50
Joudah, Fady, 9, 81

K
Kafr Yasif, 4, 51, 85
al-Karmel (journal), 8, 59, 86
Kashua, Sayed, 24, 28, 29
  Dancing Arabs, 24, 27–29, 42
Khalife, Marcel, 3, 66
al-Khal, Yusuf, 7
Khamis, Saliva, 49
Khleifi, Michel
  *Forbidden Marriages in the Holy
    Land*, 17

L
Lapidot, Ditzman Shoshana, 85, 86
leitmotif, 59, 77, 90
Liebrecht, Savyon
  "A Room on the Roof", 34, 35, 43
Lorca, 86

M
Mahfouz, Naguib, 7, 18, 54
Mara'ana-Menuhin, Ibtisam
  background of, 46
  marriage to an Israeli Jew, 47
  77 Steps, 46, 47
  Write down, I Am an Arab, 5, 46,
    48, 49, 58–59
Mattawa, Khaled, 2, 10
Mer, Arna, 49
Michael, Sami

A Trumpet in the Wadi, 34, 35,
  37–39, 43
midrash, 84
Mohammed, Zakaria, 89
al-Mutanabbi, 53

N
Nakba, 26, 46, 61n3
al-Naqqash, Raja', 58, 63
Neruda, Pablo, 50
Nye, Naomi Shihab
  Habibi, 33, 43

O
Oslo Accords, 8, 34, 54, 59, 76, 89
Oz, Amos
  Nomad and Viper, 34, 43

P
Palestine
  in Arabic fiction, 19–21, 24–25
  in Darwish's poetry, 2, 3, 6, 9, 67,
    68, 76, 90
Palestine Liberation Organization
  (PLO), 7, 8, 54, 55, 56, 57, 72,
  76
Peleg, Michal, 35
  "The Good Jewess", 34, 35, 43
Penn, Alexander, 50

Q
Qabbani, Rana, 54
Qais and Laila (Majnun Laila), 78, 79
al-Qasim, Samih, 4, 55, 87

R
Rabinyan, Dorit
  All the Rivers, 34, 35, 36–37, 43
  and relationship with Hassan
    Hourani, 37, 43n46

INDEX **105**

Ramadan, Somaya
  Leaves of Narcissus, 18, 42
romance across ethno-religious lines.
    See also Arab-Jewish mixed
    marriages
  between Arabs and Jews in Israel,
    14–17, 34–35, 46–47, 49
  between Arabs and Westerners,
    17–19
  between Christian Arabs and Muslim
    Arabs, 14, 17–18
  depictions of, in Arabic fiction,
    17–25, 32–34
  depictions of, in Hebrew fiction,
    26–32, 34–40
  during the Troubles in Northern
    Ireland, 14
  hardships encountered in, 17, 39, 40
  lens for examining core issues in
    Arab-Jewish relations, 34
  social attitudes of Arabs and Jews
    toward, 14–17
  success or failure of, as metaphor for
    Arab-Jewish relations, 90
  viewed as taboo in many societies,
    13, 14
Romeo and Juliet, 25, 36, 65–66, 78,
    79

S
Saleh, Tayyib
  Season of Migration to the North, 18
Salovey, Peter, 60–61, 89, 93
Sarid, Yossi, 59, 88

self-defining memories, 45, 60, 89
al-Shahham, Abdullah, 12n40, 58, 63
Shamir, Yitzhak, 55
al-Shaykh, Hanan, 19
Shipler, David, 17, 41
Shu'un Filastiniyya (journal), 8, 54
Sikseck, Ayman
  To Jaffa, 24, 29–30, 42
Singer, Jefferson A., 60–61, 89, 93
Smooha, Sammy, 15
Soueif, Ahdaf
  The Map of Love, 79, 82

T
al-Tahawy, Miral
  Brooklyn Heights, 19, 42
Tamer, Zakaria, 18
Toubi, Tawfiq, 4, 48
Touma, Emile, 4, 48, 49
Touma, Haya, 49
Tuqan, Fadwa, 88, 92
Tuqan, Fawwaz, x, 80n2, 96
Turki, Fawaz, 88, 92

W
watan, 3
Wedde, Ian, x, 80n2, 96

Y
Yehoshua, A.B.
  The Lover, 34, 35, 43
Yeshurun, Helit, 48, 53, 57, 62, 86, 91

CPSIA information can be obtained
at www.ICGtesting.com
Printed in the USA
LVHW081016101119
636873LV00014B/1564/P